£47.50

D1394495

The Critical Assessment of Research

CHANDOS
INFORMATION PROFESSIONAL SERIES

Series Editor: Ruth Rikowski
(e-mail: Rikowskigr@aol.com)

Chandos' new series of books are aimed at the busy information professional. They have been specially commissioned to provide the reader with an authoritative view of current thinking. They are designed to provide easy-to-read and (most importantly) practical coverage of topics that are of interest to librarians and other information professionals. If you would like a full listing of current and forthcoming titles, please visit our website at www.chandospublishing.com or e-mail info@chandospublishing.com or telephone +44 (0) 1223 499140.

New authors: we are always pleased to receive ideas for new titles; if you would like to write a book for Chandos, please contact Dr Glyn Jones on e-mail gjones@chandospublishing.com or telephone number +44 (0) 1993 848726.

Bulk orders: some organisations buy a number of copies of our books. If you are interested in doing this, we would be pleased to discuss a discount. Please e-mail info@chandospublishing.com or telephone +44 (0) 1223 499140.

The Critical Assessment of Research: Traditional and new methods of evaluation

ALAN BAILIN
AND
ANN GRAFSTEIN

CP
CHANDOS
PUBLISHING

Oxford Cambridge New Delhi

Chandos Publishing
TBAC Business Centre
Avenue 4
Station Lane
Witney
Oxford OX28 4BN
UK
Tel: +44 (0) 1993 848726
Email: info@chandospublishing.com
www.chandospublishing.com

Chandos Publishing is an imprint of Woodhead Publishing Limited

Woodhead Publishing Limited
80 High Street
Sawston
Cambridge CB22 3HJ
UK
Tel: +44 (0) 1223 499140
Fax: +44 (0) 1223 832819
www.woodheadpublishing.com

First published in 2010

ISBN:
978 1 84334 543 5

British Library Cataloguing-in-Publication Data.
A catalogue record for this book is available from the British Library.

Typeset in the UK by Concerto.
Printed in the UK and USA.

Printed in the UK by 4edge Limited - www.4edge.co.uk

Contents

About the authors

Alan Bailin is associate professor of library services at Hofstra University. He has a BA in anthropology and an MA and PhD in English from McGill University, as well as an MLS from Queens College, City University of New York. Prior to his present position he has held university positions at the University of Western Ontario, Texas A&M at Corpus Christie and Baruch College, City University of New York. He has been an associate editor for *Computers and the Humanities*, and a reviewer for both the National Science Foundation and the Social Sciences and Humanities Research Council of Canada. Among his many publications are 'Online tutorials, narratives and scripts' (*Journal of Academic Librarianship*, 2007), recognized as a Library Instruction Round Table 'Top Twenty' article, 'The evolution of academic libraries: the networked environment' (*Journal of Academic Librarianship*, 2005), 'The linguistic assumptions underlying readability formulae' (*Journal of Language and Communication*, 2001) and a book entitled *Metaphor and the Logic of Language Use* (Legas, 1998).

Ann Grafstein is associate professor of library services at Hofstra University. She holds a BA in French from Bryn Mawr College, a PhD in linguistics from McGill University and an MLIS from the University of Western Ontario. Prior to her present position she taught linguistics at both McGill University and the University of Western Ontario, and served as an academic librarian at Texas A&M University at Kingsville and the College of Staten Island, City University of New York. Her publications include 'Information literacy and technology: an examination of some issues' (*portal: Libraries and the Academy*, 2007), 'The evolution of academic libraries: the networked environment' (*Journal of Academic Librarianship*, 2005), 'A discipline-based approach to information literacy' (*Journal of Academic Librarianship*,

2002) and 'The linguistic assumptions underlying readability formulae' (*Journal of Language and Communication*, 2001). In 2004 she received the prestigious Association of College and Research Libraries Instruction Section Publication Award for 'A discipline-based approach to information literacy'.

Acknowledgements

We argue throughout this book that research does not take place in a vacuum. This work is no exception. Professor Bobbie Pollard read through the entire manuscript and the authors have benefited from her fresh perspectives and insightful suggestions. We are deeply indebted to our colleague, Professor Martha Kreisel, for her professional, meticulous and skillful work on the bibliographical references.

On a more personal note, Ann's mother, Eleanor Grafstein, offered an enthusiastic and interested ear as well as a healthy and encouraging dose of cheerleading. We are grateful to our daughters, Naomi and Rebecca Bailin, both for putting up with our sometimes obsessive behaviors in the preparation of this book and for reminding us from time to time of the world outside. It is to these intelligent young women that we dedicate this book.

Introduction

Research is an integral part of our world. It is responsible for, among other things, the medicines that we take, our economic policies, our approaches to marketing, the educational strategies used in our schools, therapeutic strategies for the mentally distressed and the techniques for harnessing energy for industry. This book is about evaluating research. It is about assessing studies that have shaped our lives in fundamental ways.

Research is to a great extent the domain of experts and specialists: scientists hired by governments and industries, professors in universities, PhDs working for foundations or in research centers. This book, however, is not for them, at least not in so far as they are experts. It does not discuss the fine points of evaluating the internal consistency of theories, nor the empirical coverage of different kinds of theoretical models. As important as all of these discussions are for the specialists engaged in research, they are not within the domain of this book.

This book is for the rest of us: those of us who read about research but are not experts in the field. It is for those of us who search for ways of understanding important ideas and try to identify poorly thought-out proposals in areas in which we have some interest or concerns, but in which we have not been trained to be specialists. Since even experts are only experts in limited areas, this means that this book is for all of us.

All of us need ways to assess the research findings we encounter. Whether we are reading about the newest medical discoveries, trying to decide where to invest our money, considering the proposals of politicians for the development of new energy resources – in all of those many areas in which research and research findings affect our lives and we have no way of making an expert assessment – all of us need a basic knowledge of what to look for, and what to look out for.

When research is reported in popular media outlets, its findings are often presented as established facts, and even sometimes as a clarion call for immediate action. Nevertheless, it sometimes turns out that these calls to action are based on questionable research. In the 1990s, for example, menopausal women were urged by such reputable sources as the American Heart Association (Felgran and Hettinger, 2002: 71) and the American College of Physicians (Kolata and Petersen, 2002) to have hormone replacement therapy (HRT) in order to decrease the chances of developing heart disease and osteoporosis. By 2002 HRT was viewed far more skeptically as a result of later findings: while it indeed lowered the risk of osteoporosis, at the same time it increased the risk of stroke, heart disease, breast cancer and dementia (Writing Group for the Women's Health Initiative Investigators, 2002).

The financial sphere is another example of an area where information, even when disseminated from reputable sources, requires close scrutiny. Enron was considered one of the fastest-growing companies and a safe investment. Anyone researching the company found reassuring financial statements based on apparently impeccable accounting research. Nevertheless, the collapse of Enron became worldwide news. It might be tempting to think that the Enron situation is an aberration, but the accounting conflicts of interest that contributed to it have been widespread (Fearnley et al., 2005: 69).

The intention of the book is to present the reader with some of the basic concepts that can be used for assessing the quality of research, regardless of its topic or area of specialization. It tries to point the reader to warning flags that ought to prompt further questions and perhaps some skepticism. In sum, this book is about assessing research as a non-expert in an intelligent, educated manner.

There are tried-and-true methods of deciding whether particular research is worth even considering. In the second chapter we discuss these criteria, showing why they are used and pointing out where they can be useful. However, we also show you where these criteria fall short, and why trusting these gold standards as the primary criteria for assessing research can lead to misplaced confidence.

In Chapters 3–5 we look at issues that can affect the validity of research. In particular, we look at questions related to the funding of research, the theoretical models upon which the research is based and the venues available for disseminating it. In each case we investigate the way in which economic and ideological systems can affect research and its outcomes.

In the third chapter we examine the issues of funding and sponsorship. We show how the sources that fund and sponsor research may affect its outcomes and conclusions. In so doing, we look at three different cases in quite different fields. First we examine the ways in which pharmaceutical funding and sponsorship of drug-related research have affected the way in which the findings of that research are viewed. We look at how pharmaceutical companies used funding to spin the research evidence to make hormone replacement therapies appear safer than the research might have otherwise suggested.

Next, we look at the Enron debacle to see how funding conflicts of interest can corrupt the investigations of auditors (in other words, their research) into a company's financial health. We discuss how funding played a decisive role in corrupting the auditing of Enron's financial status and thus allowed Enron to produce flawed financial reports – reports that were nevertheless thought to be sound because the auditors had investigated Enron's reporting practices and approved them.

We then move to the field of psychology and the appearance of a much-heralded book, *The Bell Curve*, which claimed to establish racial differences in IQ scores. Although it might seem that the funding of research would relate solely to economic self-interest, *The Bell Curve* illustrates how funding can be used to promote ideological agendas as well. We discuss how one of the authors was supported by foundations that have specific ideological agendas. We address the convergence between the agendas of the funding sources and the findings of the research. Our interest is not in whether or not the book's conclusions are 'true' or offensive, but rather whether or not this convergence should prompt questions about the research.

While financial conflicts of interest are the stuff of which magazine and newspaper articles are often made, there are other considerations which are far subtler but can nevertheless affect the nature of research. In the fourth chapter we look at research from the perspective of how dominant research models (paradigms) exert influence not only over the conclusions of research studies, but even over the questions that are asked, the hypotheses that are investigated and the subjects that are studied. Theoretical paradigms constitute the set of assumptions – that is ideas – that form the framework within which research takes place. The focus of the fourth chapter is thus on the relationship between ideological systems and research.

We look first at one of the most influential research applications around the world, IQ tests, and show that the research supporting the use of these tests and the claim that they identify inheritable traits depends on particular theoretical assumptions. Different assumptions, we suggest, lead to different conclusions about intelligence and the meaning of its inheritability. We argue that an awareness of alternative perspectives is important in critically evaluating this research.

The next case we look at involves the causes of ulcers. Research throughout much of the twentieth century was based on a theoretical model that emphasized the role of stress in the development of ulcers. Treatment regimens were routinely recommended on the basis of this assumption. But late in the twentieth century a radically different theoretical model of ulcers was proposed. This model met with considerable resistance because it differed substantially from the dominant theoretical paradigm. Nevertheless, the newer model eventually gained acceptance because it led to more effective treatments. In science, accepted paradigms are periodically overthrown and replaced. In critically assessing research, we suggest, it is prudent to keep in mind that theories that seem far-fetched today may become the established truth of tomorrow.

Science is hardly the only area in which dominant paradigms affect research. In our final case study in this chapter we look at the effect of canons on research topics in the humanities and fine arts. We show how for years the focus of the Anglo-American literary canon meant that little research investigated anyone but British male writers. In recent years academicians have discovered, however, that there was serious literature created by a far more diverse group of writers, whose work had been ignored because it was not part of the canon. A similar trend can be found in the area of fine arts, and we discuss this with particular reference to female artists. We discuss how the canon discourages research into subjects that are excluded from it.

In Chapter 5 we turn to the dissemination of research. In the first case study we show that since the second half of the twentieth century there has been an explosion of journals created by groups that did not view themselves as adequately represented by mainstream journals, frequently because of ideological reasons. The fields of women's studies and gay studies developed to address the intellectual needs of groups that were struggling for power. Academic journals were started in order to publish and disseminate research on topics of specific interest to these emerging fields of study. We point out that when assessing research in these areas, it is important to consider research from these newer publication venues. Considering publications that offer new and different perspectives on topics, we suggest, provides a more complete context for critically assessing research.

In the next case study we focus on the effects of economic rather than ideological interests. We consider instances in which pharmaceutical companies sponsoring research have influenced its dissemination. We show that sponsorship has sometimes led to the cherry-picking of the data that are reported and even the outright suppression of research findings.

Finally, we look at the ways in which governments, foundations, corporations and other institutions support and disseminate research in what is known as 'gray literature'. We show that gray literature often fills the gaps left by traditional publication venues. These gaps may be the result of either economics or ideology; in either case gray literature provides access to research that may not be disseminated in other ways. As with the new journals, gray literature can thus provide a perspective that would otherwise be missing when we critically assess research.

In the sixth and final chapter we discuss practical ways to go beyond the gold standards for evaluating research and find the information you need to make sound assessments. We suggest ways to track down the funding sources of research and find out about alternative publication venues and different research paradigms, using both print and digital resources. Much of this information is available for free on the web and in libraries, and we show you how to use these resources efficiently and effectively. We conclude by discussing how to strike the appropriate balance in the critical assessment of research, viewing research with a skeptical eye without rejecting the important information and perspectives it can provide.

2

The gold standards

Introduction

If you are not an expert in a field of research, how are you going to evaluate the reliability of research findings? As we said in the Introduction, this is not an abstract or theoretical question, of importance only to scientists and other scholars who care about research for a living. The mass media (television, radio, newspapers, magazines and, more recently, internet sites) disseminate major research findings, since they are of interest to and have significant implications for the general public. We base many of our most important decisions on reports about research. Sometimes this research gives us good information and sometimes it does not. Sometimes what research seems to tell us we find out later is just plain wrong, even dangerous.

In the first chapter we mentioned research about hormone replacement therapy (HRT), and pointed out that in the 1990s medical research seemed to suggest that HRT could help prevent heart disease and osteoporosis. HRT was routinely prescribed for healthy menopausal women, based on the assumption that it would protect them from both osteoporosis and heart disease. However, by 2002 further research suggested that this apparently effective treatment was not nearly as safe as had been previously thought. HRT was found to be implicated in heart disease, breast cancer and even dementia (Palmlund, 2006).

What are people who are not experts to make of such reversals? Research indicates a certain course of action, expert practitioners – in this case medical doctors – act on this research, and then it turns out that the research was at best misleading if not simply wrong. How can an intelligent, educated person make sense of it all? Is it best to trust absolutely nothing? Alternatively, should we simply have faith in the research and hope all works out for the best?

Peer review

Clearly we need to be able to assess research critically. In many, perhaps most, cases, all we have to go on is what we read or hear about research, and often what we read or hear is second-hand information reported in the mass media. However, although at times researchers make themselves available for interviews and sometimes even give press conferences, almost all research is only fully presented in specialized peer-reviewed journals or books intended for experts in the field.

The key term here is 'peer review', and it is perhaps the most important of the gold-standard criteria for evaluating research. It is essential to understand what 'peer review' means, the pivotal role it plays in the dissemination of research and its significance as a tool for assessment by non-experts.

Peer review is basically a selection process. When scientists or scholars have research findings they want to present, or when they want to discuss other researchers' findings, they generally submit a manuscript to a book publisher or the editor of a journal that publishes that kind of research (Bakanic et al., 1987). In either case the manuscript is sent to experts in the field. These experts (the peers) review the work and make recommendations about whether or not it should be published. In addition, they often make suggestions for revisions that the author(s) must make before the work is published. At least in theory, these reviews are based primarily on the strength of the arguments and the supporting evidence, as well as the extent to which the article contributes to the knowledge base of the field.

Peer review plays a decisive role in the professional lives of scholars and scientists: those who are unable to navigate successfully through the peer-review process have short careers. But what does peer review mean for the non-expert consumer of research? To a great extent, it is relevant to us because it is the single most important criterion that can help us distinguish between works which scientists and scholars look at as serious research and works which are not looked on in that way. If a researcher cannot get his or her work published in a peer-reviewed publication, there is a good chance that it is not something worth considering.

Graduate students are often taught to use peer-reviewed publications because they are considered to be more authoritative sources than even serious popular magazines such as *The Economist* and *Scientific American*. The instruction is not always explicit: it does not need to be.

Suggested readings in syllabi, for example, as well as all the citations contained within these readings generally include nothing but peer-reviewed materials. An examination of the citations in scientific or scholarly publications suggests that when these students become researchers themselves they rarely if ever use sources that are not peer reviewed. Moreover, as graduate students become professionals, they learn that publication in peer-reviewed outlets is essential for achieving tenure and promotion in academia or career advancement in scientific research labs.

That said, peer review does not function in the same way in all contexts. It is worth noting, for example, that one of the primary research activities performed in the business sphere – that is, accounting reports of financial performances of publicly owned companies – does not use the standard peer-review process. Rather, accounting reports follow the standards and guidelines set by oversight boards (see, for example, American Institute of Certified Public Accountants, 2009b, 2009c; Financial Reporting Council, 2009a). Still, auditors of public companies are subject to oversight. In the United States, for example, they are subject to mandatory peer review (Public Oversight Board, 2001; American Institute of Certified Public Accountants, 2009a; see also Financial Reporting Council, 2009b). Such oversight can be considered similar in conception to the peer-review process in other fields.

It should be noted that research published in books does not necessarily go through the same process as articles published in journals. While peer review in journals is generally focused strictly on the quality of the research (see, for example, *Journal of English for Academic Purposes*, 2009), peer review of research for books also often considers marketability (Routledge, Taylor & Francis Group, 2007; Thompson, 2005: 45–6). Nevertheless, no matter the field or the publication venue, serious research work is always subject to review by other professionals in the field, and this review is perhaps the most basic standard to ensure the quality of research.

Publisher reputation

In addition to peer review, the reputation of the publisher is often applied as a metric in assessing the quality of research. Certain publishing houses are recognized as publishing quality books; journals, too, are accorded greater prestige if they are published by a reputable publishing company – a university press, for example – than they are if they are published by an unknown or poorly regarded company (see, for example, Thompson, 2005: 32). So, for example, one could argue that the *Urban Library Journal* is a rather obscure journal without much prestige in part because it is published by a rather small in-house organization within the City University of New York, while the *Journal of Academic Librarianship* and *portal: Libraries and the Academy* are more highly regarded because the former is published by the well-regarded scholarly and academic publisher Elsevier and the latter by Johns Hopkins University Press.

In some cases at least, there can be little doubt that the reputation of a publisher should be considered in assessing the authority of a work. For example, research published by a vanity press, in which the author pays for the publication of the work, should be looked at with some skepticism, if only because publication by a vanity press usually indicates that no other publisher was interested in the work, presumably at least in part because of its intellectual content. A work published by a vanity press, moreover, has not been subjected to the peer-review process.

Author credentials

Perhaps even more important than the reputation of the publisher are the credentials and reputation of the researcher. Does the author have credentials in the field in which he or she is writing? What determines an author's authority with respect to a field is not simply possession of, say, a PhD or affiliation with a university. Rather, if an author is to be recognized as having the authority to disseminate research in a particular field, his or her credentials should normally be in that field (see the treatment of cognitive authority in Wilson, 1983, especially Chapter 2). While Dr Laura Schlessinger has achieved popularity as a pop psychologist on American radio, her books are not taken seriously as psychological research. No doubt one of the reasons for this is that she has a doctorate in physiology but no credentials whatsoever in psychology itself, only a license in marriage and family therapy (Lilienfeld, 2002: 187; *Marquis Who's Who on the Web*, 2009).

Similarly, Holocaust deniers, while presenting their work as scholarly, have frequently had either education in fields unrelated to their Holocaust works or no professional credentials whatsoever. Thus Arthur Butz, one of the leading Holocaust deniers, is a professor of engineering and computer science at Northwestern University, but has no expertise at all in historical research (Lipstadt, 1993: Chapter 7), while David Irving, a well-known writer of histories often sympathetic to the Nazis, has no college degree at all (Duff, 2006). The lack of appropriate qualifications has without doubt made it more difficult for them to present their work as serious research.

Gold standards and the mass media

There are then certain gold standards that are commonly used to evaluate research. The first of these is the peer-review process, which is intended to ensure that only research that passes the scrutiny of recognized scholars in the field is published. The second gold standard is the reputation of the publisher, which is a factor in determining how the scholarship is received. Finally, the evaluation of research is affected by the credentials of the author: an author who has recognized expertise in a field is considered to have authority to write in that field.

How widely accepted are these gold standards? Even mass-media publications – newspapers and popular magazines – in discussions of research often make particular note that the research was published in a peer-reviewed publication as an important indicator of its credibility. In a *New York Times* article on research on cold fusion, for example, peer review is mentioned as a prime measure of scientific worthiness by James F. Decker, deputy director of the Science Office in the US Department of Energy:

> Dr. Decker said the department was open to proposals for cold fusion research, but added that was not new. 'We have always been open to proposals that have scientific merit as determined by peer review,' he said. (Chang, 2004)

As part of an attempt to show, it would seem, the seriousness of the research, a *New York Daily News* article notes that a researcher claiming a link between cancer and cell phones will be submitting his findings to peer review in a journal:

> Khurana, who has received 14 awards in the past 16 years for his scholarship, has submitted his findings to a scientific journal for peer review. (Goldiner, 2008)

The London newspaper *The Independent*, in reporting that Pfizer is trying to undermine the peer-review process, notes as a simple uncontroversial fact the importance of peer review:

> A multinational drugs company is trying to force a medical science journal to reveal the confidential statements made by the journal's expert reviewers in a test case that could undermine one of the central tenets of the scientific process. (Connor, 2008)

Even *Christianity Today*, a religious magazine, notes the importance of peer review in discussing scientific validity:

> Yes, archaeologists – professional and amateur – are still making discoveries, but their pronouncements must meet a basic standard of verification. In the scientific world that's called the peer review process. (Govier, 2008)

Journal reputation is also touted in the mass media, albeit in a somewhat subtler manner. Journals of high prestige are often mentioned, it would seem, to underscore the validity of the research reported. Consider the way the following selection from a CNN news report cites the journal *Nature* as an authoritative source:

> One-third of all children who attend public schools in the United States are being taught unsatisfactory science, according to a study published today in the journal *Nature*. (Environmental News Network, 2000)

More explicitly, the *New York Times* notes that a report on Vioxx was published 'in a leading medical journal *JAMA*' (Saul, 2008). Here, too, the intent would appear to be to add credibility to the report by associating it with the prestige of the journal.

The credentials of the researcher are also often mentioned in the mass media to lend credibility to the findings, as in the following quote from a Montreal newspaper:

> 'We now have six very large trials of statin use (cholesterol-lowering drugs) in patients with heart disease, and these studies have more than 100,000 people in them, and in none of these studies where the cholesterol was lowered tremendously is there an increase in heart failure,' said Jacques Genest, head of cardiology

at Montreal's McGill University and a spokesperson for the Heart and Stroke Foundation. (Kirkey, 2006)

In a similar manner, the credentials of an archeologist are noted to give weight to his claims:

> 'The geographical location of Oymaagaç, the impressive representative building on top of the acropolis, and especially the tiny cuneiform writing style on the tablet fragments all suggested the excavators might find Nerik here,' said Thomas Zimmerman, representative from Ankara's Bilkent University and acting chair of the department of archeology and history of art. (Çimen, 2008)

Sometimes the credentials are noted in a rather matter-of-fact manner:

> Dr Jim Provan, from Queen's School of Biological Sciences, said the climate change adaptation is a rare example of good news. 'Our results, in contrast to previous studies, suggest the species were able to respond to previous changes in the Earth's climate, and thus "track" the effects of climate change, a feature which may be crucial in its survival,' he said. (McKee, 2008)

Limitations of the gold standards

We can see that the three gold standards – peer review, the reputation of the publisher and journal, and the researcher's credentials – are used not only by the scholarly and scientific community but also by the mass media. And through the mass media, whether we are aware of it or not, the use of these standards affects all of us. We find out much of what we know through these media and use this information to make judgements.

It would be difficult to argue that the gold standards are not useful. Very few of us would want to take research findings seriously if they were not able to pass muster with other experts. Nor would we want to take the conclusions of someone with no expertise in a field of knowledge seriously. In addition, as we pointed out earlier, we might also be suspicious with good reason if no respectable publisher or journal wanted to publish the research results. Clearly the gold standards play an important role.

But let us go back to where this chapter started – that is, with the research on hormone replacement therapy for women. At first, the research suggested that HRT was beneficial. Later research suggested that in addition to the benefits, HRT poses serious dangers. Nevertheless, all of the research met the gold standards. It was peer reviewed; the research was published in very respectable publications; the researchers had appropriate credentials.

Can we simply attribute the difference in the research results to the sometimes twisted paths research must take? Without doubt, there are occasions, possibly many occasions, when the best investigations of any particular issue lead to conclusions which later turn out to be wrong. The history of science is filled with such examples. Only with the discovery of microorganisms did people begin to think that small living things were the cause of infection (Magner, 1992: 305ff). Before the Copernican revolution it was generally thought that the sun revolved around the earth (Rabin, 2005). With this in mind, it is perhaps best to maintain a certain degree of skepticism about whatever we think must be absolutely true.

The idea that even the most widely accepted theories supported by the most rigorous research will at some point be supplanted by other theories with the development of new knowledge is not controversial. Still, beyond this, are there times when we should be skeptical about research that has been subjected to the peer-review process, undertaken by highly qualified researchers and disseminated in reputable publications? Was there anything that might have suggested that there should have been extra skepticism about the original hormone replacement research? We will argue in the following chapters that in the case of HRT research, as well as in many other cases, there are factors that are extraneous to the research itself – in particular economic and ideological interests – that can influence the research process and its conclusions.

There is nothing really new about this. One of the most famous cases of extraneous factors affecting research was that of the Catholic Church and Galileo. Galileo created a telescope in 1609 and used it to find data that supported the hypothesis that the planets, including the earth, revolve around the sun. After publishing a book which offered research evidence supporting the theory, the Catholic Church's Inquisition charged Galileo with heresy and found him guilty. The famous scientist was forced to recant his research findings publicly and produce revised findings that agreed with the Church (Machamer, 2009).

A less well-known recantation took place in the eighteenth century. The French geologist Georges Buffon published a book entitled *L'Histoire Naturelle* (*Natural History*) that argued the earth's surface was continually being transformed. The Sorbonne's Faculty of Theology vigorously opposed this research contention and argued that it contradicted biblical teachings. Because of threats to his career, Buffon was forced to recant his contention (Gruber, 1974).

These historical cases involve rather obvious, even clumsy, efforts to corrupt and suppress the research process. As we will see, in many instances the ways in which research is affected by external influences are not quite so visible. In Chapters 3–5 we provide examples of how economic and ideological considerations can negatively influence research and its outcomes, on occasion in ways that only became clear years after the initial research was made public. We will show how these examples can help us to ask questions about motivations and funding, about context and goals – questions that might not otherwise occur to us but that can help us to assess modern research in a more sensible and critically aware manner.

3

Sponsorship and funding

Introduction

Research requires funding: researchers, unless they are very wealthy, need to earn a living, and research itself generally requires tools and materials that are rarely free of charge. Funding is therefore generally necessary, and it should come as no surprise that those who provide the funding for the research often have interests in the findings. Given such interests, it should also come as no surprise that those who provide the funding sometimes try to use their position to influence the research process or the way in which the findings are interpreted.

The first two cases we discuss in this chapter illustrate how the economic interests of funders can influence both the way research findings are viewed and the findings themselves. In the first case we examine in greater detail the hormone replacement therapy research mentioned in the first two chapters. We look at how the pharmaceutical companies used their influence as funders to affect what research was promoted, what research was ignored and how research was interpreted. We then examine the Enron scandal and see how accounting reports on Enron's business performance presented flawed data and so helped to hide the problems with Enron's business model. Accounting reports are verified by independent audits of the financial performance of a company, and these audits can be considered one of the most basic kinds of business research. We show how flaws in these audits were likely to have been caused by economic conflicts of interest: the accounting firm which produced the audits was paid for both the audits and other services by the very company it was supposed to be investigating.

The third and final case we discuss in this chapter illustrates another way in which funding should prompt us to look critically at research. This time, an examination of funding points to ideological issues rather than economic conflicts of interest. In the case of *The Bell Curve*, the concern is not that the funders tried to influence unduly the research for economic reasons; rather, the clear ideological agendas of the funding sources suggest that the researchers themselves approached the research with ideological biases that may have compromised the integrity of their work.

These are the broad outlines of what we will be discussing. The devils, however, are in the details.

Case 1: hormone replacement therapy

When we think of conflicts of interest related to funding, our thoughts probably turn first to the possibility of funders interfering with the research process itself. Our first case, however, relates not to the research process, but to something less obvious and thus potentially more insidious: the way in which research findings are interpreted, not only as individual studies, but also in relation to other research.

In the last chapter we referred to research findings that led to a reassessment of the risks and benefits of HRT. These newer research findings changed the way the medical profession and the public regarded HRT. Rather than simply an effective and benign antidote to osteoporosis and heart disease, HRT came to be seen as a potentially dangerous therapy. At first glance it would seem that researchers simply learned more about the therapy, and because of the new findings the value of the therapy was reassessed. Closer examination makes clear, however, that this was not the case – there were, in fact, warning signs before the more recent research, and these warning signs were ignored. In the following discussion of HRT, we will see how the economic agendas of the companies that sponsored the HRT research played a prominent role in creating the positive assessment that flowed from the earlier research.

Estrogen, the primary component of HRT, had been given to women as far back as the 1920s:

> Since the early decades of the 20th century, estrogen drugs have been a technology in search of problems it could be applied to. Musings about the potential uses of estrogenic products and their physiological functions propelled a wave of experiments, in laboratories with animal bodies and in medical practice with

human bodies. Estrogen preparations have been given to patients as soon as doctors guessed that a lack of internally produced estrogens might be the source of physical or mental trouble. In the 1920s, doctors began giving female patients injections of distilled natural estrogens in oil solution to help women overcome discomforts associated with menopause. (Palmlund, 2006: 542)

By 1938 an article in *JAMA* (*Journal of the American Medical Association*) proclaimed the success of hormone therapy at treating a variety of menopausal symptoms (ibid.). Despite this, as far back as 1938 there was research that indicated there were cancer risks related to taking estrogen:

Pills as a safe, low-cost alternative to the injections of natural estrogens were introduced in 1938, when the synthetic estrogen diethylstilbestrol (DES) became available. The budding pharmaceutical industry immediately identified DES as an opportunity. *Despite warnings of cancer and other risks...* numerous DES products with different brand names were soon approved in many countries. (Ibid., emphasis added)

In the 1960s pharmaceutical companies made a major marketing push aimed both at the medical profession and at women. Perhaps the most famous of these promotional efforts was the book *Feminine Forever* (Wilson, 1966), written by Robert A. Wilson, a gynecologist. During the first seven months following publication, 100,000 copies were sold (Palmlund, 2006: 543). His work became so popular that it was excerpted in the high-circulation magazines *Look* and *Vogue* (ibid.). The conclusions of the book were supposed to be based on years of research by Wilson: he had published 14 articles in major medical journals in which he detailed the benefits of HRT. Nevertheless, Wilson did not hold any academic position, nor did he have experience as a clinical investigator (Rothman and Rothman, 2003: 75). How then did his work become so highly influential?

Wilson's advocacy of estrogen began with a 1962 peer-reviewed article in *JAMA* arguing that not only did estrogen not cause cancers but it might in fact help to reduce their occurrence (Wilson, 1962). Between April 1963 and August 1964 he published 13 more articles, all advocating HRT. Then in 1964 came the money: he received a research grant from three pharmaceutical companies – Ayerst Laboratories, the Searle Foundation and the Upjohn Company – all of which manufactured hormones used in HRT. The grant was given to establish the Wilson Foundation, the purpose of which was to promote the use of hormone therapy (Rothman and Rothman, 2003: 75). The role of the pharmaceutical industry in establishing Wilson's foundation was confirmed by his son, Ronald Wilson, in a 2002 *New York Times* article. In addition, Ronald Wilson stated that the Wyeth-Ayerst pharmaceutical company paid for all his father's expenses in writing *Feminine Forever* (Kolata and Petersen, 2002). It should be noted that a spokesman for Wyeth, Douglas Perkins, is reported in the *Boston Globe* as saying 'no evidence exists in company files of a financial arrangement' with Wilson (Smith, 2003). A statement that there is 'no evidence' is not, of course, the same as a simple denial, and there is no reason to think – at least at the time of this writing – that Ronald Wilson was not telling the truth.

Did Wyeth and the other pharmaceutical companies find an enthusiast in Wilson and decide to promote him, or did his enthusiasm result from financial incentives? In a very basic way, it does not matter. The simple truth is that in either case, the financial support given to Wilson, a proponent of estrogen-based therapies, contributed to a focus on positive research findings concerning HRT and a tendency to ignore research such as the Framingham Study that suggested serious – even fatal – dangers (Katz, 2003: 928; Palmlund, 2006: 544). The Framingham Study, which investigated the effects of estrogen treatment on 1,234 post-menopausal women between the ages of 50 and 83, found specifically that there was an increased risk of heart disease and stroke as a result of estrogen treatment (Wilson et al., 1985). Nevertheless, the marketing promotion of the 'positive' research was so successful that, according to the *British Medical Journal (BMJ)*, in 2001 over 100 million women used HRT (Clark, 2003), despite the fact that in 1998 a clinical study called HERS (Heart and Estrogen-progestin Replacement Study) (Hulley et al., 1998), which was sponsored by Wyeth, found 'an unexpected pattern of increased risk [of heart disease] during the first year of follow up' (Herrington, 2003: 2).

None of this is intended to suggest that the funding itself led to tainted results. If it did, the HERS study referred to above, which was fully funded by Wyeth (Dey and Constantine, 2004), should have produced positive results. However, the study found that HRT increased the occurrence of heart attacks in women who already had heart disease.

Still, the funding Wilson received certainly promoted research and research-based opinions favorable to HRT. These findings and opinions were then given far more weight than they might otherwise have had. It is significant that it was only with the Women's Health Initiative in 2002

– research completely independent of Wyeth and other pharmaceutical companies (Writing Group for the Women's Health Initiative Investigators, 2002) – that the dangers of HRT were widely disseminated (Palmlund, 2006: 546–7).

At least in one case, the sponsors of HRT research provided a 'spin' that went beyond promoting the positive and ignoring the negative. In 2003 the *BMJ* published the report of a study, funded by Wyeth, that documented an increase in the risk of dementia in elderly women as a result of the company's combined estrogen and progesterone pill (Moynihan, 2003). Wyeth admitted that it briefed medical societies about the results of this study well in advance of its publication:

> 'Under a written confidentiality agreement Wyeth medical personnel shared a limited and balanced summary report of the data with a senior medical expert at certain critical medical societies,' said Dr Victoria Kusiak, the company's North American medical director. 'These discussions were meant to allow those individuals to respond knowledgeably to their constituents, at the time the [study] data became public.' (Ibid.)

It should be noted that this leaking of the research findings well in advance of publication was a departure from the standard practice of briefing news agencies on the results of peer-reviewed articles only a few days prior to publication in order to assist them in preparing news stories. These early leaks enabled the medical societies to promote the company's public relations strategy of 'play[ing] down the significance of the findings on dementia for younger users, stressing that women in the latest study were over 65 years old' (ibid.). Here the company was using its privileged status as a funder to tamper with the normal dissemination process and thus more effectively spin explanations to mitigate the impact of damaging findings.

The problems we have discussed with the funding of HRT research are not unique. Indeed, there are reasons to look closely at industry sponsorship, particularly since such sponsorship of scientific and medical research increased dramatically during the last 20 years of the twentieth century (Warner and Gluck, 2003). More specifically, there was an increase from about $1.5 billion in 1980 to about $22 billion in 2001 of research sponsored by pharmaceutical companies, while funding by the National Institutes of Health and the National Science Foundation increased at a far slower rate (ibid.: 36).

As we have seen in the case of HRT, the effects of industry sponsorship can be considerable. In fact, they may go beyond the kind of 'spin' we have seen in the HRT case. One investigation, for example, suggests that 'studies sponsored by for-profit companies are more likely to report results favorable to the effectiveness of their own products than are studies from other funding sources [and]... less likely than other studies to report unfavorable outcomes...' (ibid.: 39).

Clearly, industry sponsorship of research should at the very least raise the yellow flag of caution. When we critically assess research, it should make us aware of the way funders can use their position to make the research appear to say what they want it to say.

Case 2: Enron

Our second case examines a way in which funding can actually influence research itself. Here we are concerned not with the way the research findings are reported and interpreted, but rather with the findings themselves and the way in which the perceived economic self-interest of the researchers can cause them to produce findings that they think will please their funders. What better place to look for such clear conflicts of interest than in the area of business, where the profit motive is paramount?

Business depends crucially on sound financial data. For this reason many businesses, as well as colleges and universities that offer business programs, license business database products such as Mergent Online, Business Source Premier and Business & Company Resource Center, which offer a variety of financial data. Analyses of both industries and specific companies, whether in newspapers or scholarly journals, crucially depend on such data. Perhaps most importantly, the decisions of investors both large and small, as well as government policy-makers, are often based at least in part on financial information. Its integrity is therefore of the utmost importance. Accounting auditors are supposed to ensure the soundness of the data that are reported by investigating and assessing the financial reporting of a company to see if it follows acceptable practice.

Nevertheless, in the last few decades a number of scandals have made it clear that financial data are not always sound. One of these, the Enron scandal, provides a case study in how funding issues that impact the economic self-interest of the investigators can corrupt auditors' findings

– findings that are supposed to be based on investigating the integrity and soundness of the company's financial reporting.

Enron began life when the Northern Natural Gas Company bought Houston Natural Gas in 1985. In 1986 the new company changed its name to Enron. The merger of the two companies resulted in the second-largest pipeline system in the United States and the first natural gas pipeline that was national in scope (Anderson, 2002: 27). Within two years it was already encountering troubles. The unauthorized activities of traders in its New York office led to an $85 million charge against earnings in the fall of 1987 when the activities came to light (Chandra, 2003: 101).

There were some aspects to this debacle which clearly foreshadowed the much larger scandal that occurred years later. Enron's New York traders used two sets of books in order to conceal their fraudulent trading (ibid.). They set up bogus entities to create financial transactions that misrepresented the actual financial situation of the company. These manipulations may well have made Enron's finances appear to be in better shape than they actually were and enabled the company to meet the financial requirements of debt obligations. Nevertheless, since the debacle appeared to be the work of renegade traders, it did not impact on the reputation of Enron, especially since the traders fraudulently enriched themselves in the process, a fact that allowed Enron to file suits against these traders (Eichenwald, 2005: 34–9).

Enron grew with a wide variety of ventures, including some outside the United States. In 1988 it opened a wholly owned subsidiary in the United Kingdom (Anderson, 2002: 25). In 1992 it acquired Transportadora de Gas del Sur SA, a southern Argentina pipeline system operator (ibid.: 26). In 1993 it started operating a power plant in Great Britain (ibid.). In the same year it also partnered with General Electric and Bechtel to construct a power plant in Dabhol, India (Chandra, 2003: 101). In 1994 it formed a new company, Enron Global Power and Pipelines, for 'developing-nation projects' (Anderson, 2002: 28).

Meanwhile, it was also very busy on the domestic front. It developed the idea of a 'gas bank': instead of simply supplying natural gas to customers, Enron's gas bank would function as an intermediary between suppliers and buyers (Healy and Palepu, 2003: 6). Enron offered long-term contracts and reduced its exposure to price fluctuations by using financial derivatives and off-the-books financing involving 'special purpose entities' (ibid.) – that is, 'entities created by a sponsoring company for a limited purpose, such as to hold a particular asset' (US Senate Committee on Governmental Affairs, 2002: 25, note 77). These innovations helped Enron to become very successful; by 1992 it was the largest North American natural gas merchant (Healy and Palepu, 2003: 6).

Enron used its natural gas model to become a financial trader in many other areas, perhaps most notably electric power. By the end of 1997 the Enron Capital and Trade Resources division had become 'the nation's largest wholesale buyer and seller of natural gas and electricity' (Thomas, 2002). In addition, Enron developed Enron Online in 1999, a website for commodities trading that made it a party to all financial transactions performed on the website (ibid.).

Enron's apparent success led its stock price to soar. Nevertheless, in 2001 energy prices started to fall and this had a negative effect on Enron's profitability (ibid.). After this, the unravelling of Enron came about rather swiftly.

Suspicions about its financial reporting started to arise. Enron had used the special purpose entities for years not only as a vehicle for facilitating its financial transactions but also to 'reduce its debt to total assets ratio' (ibid.) – that is, to make it seem as though Enron had less debt than it actually had relative to its worth. It accomplished this by moving its debt to these special purpose entities in ways which, to say the least, were questionable. Enron noted their use in its 2000 annual report, but it did so in a way that led analysts to question whether Enron was forthcoming in its financial reporting (ibid.).

Then Enron began to report losses not only for the current fiscal period but also by revising its earnings statements for previous years. After reporting its first losses in four years in its third-quarter earnings statement of October 2001 (Anderson, 2002: 19; Thomas, 2002), it proceeded in November to revise its reported 1999 and 2000 earnings downward by $95 million and $8 million respectively (Chandra, 2003: 104). The business situation did not get any better, and by December Enron was in bankruptcy and had laid off over 4,000 workers (Anderson, 2002: 18).

The rise and fall of Enron were inextricably bound up with financial reporting. Inaccurate positive income reports provided the credibility it needed to sustain its positive credit ratings and continue its expansion. Reports about financial losses and inaccurate and/or misleading accounting of its finances hastened Enron's demise. In both the first relatively small scandal of 1987 and the enormous debacle of 2001, the accounting firm of Arthur Andersen was an auditor (Eichenwald, 2005: 34–9; Anderson, 2002: 19). In neither case did the accounting firm blow any whistles.

Andersen's report about the earlier scandal said nothing about the bogus partners or forged documents that the traders created (Eichenwald, 2005: 36). In relation to the far larger and more serious scandal of 2001, the report of a special committee of Enron's board of directors noted that 'Andersen did not fulfill its professional responsibilities in connection with its audits of Enron's financial statements, or its obligation to bring to the attention of Enron's Board (or the Audit and Compliance Committee) concerns about Enron's internal controls over the related-party transactions' (Powers Report, as quoted in US Senate Committee on Governmental Affairs, 2002: 27). In fact, as a report of the staff to the United States Senate Committee on Governmental Affairs points out, 'Andersen helped structure many of the transactions Enron used to improve the appearance of its financial statements but which had no economic purpose' (ibid.). Moreover, it appears that Andersen was quite aware of the questionable nature of the transactions (ibid.: 28).

Given the crucial role accounting reports play in making financial decisions, the stature Arthur Andersen had enjoyed and the seriousness of the lapses in its auditing reports, the question of what went wrong with the oversight and reporting process is of the utmost importance. The heart of the issue would seem to be in some ways similar to that of the problematic pharmaceutical research: economic self-interest in both cases seems to have led to a desire to misrepresent findings. However, in this case the misrepresentation took a different form. Instead of the funders attempting to 'spin' the findings, the researcher – that is the auditing company, Andersen – took it upon itself to produce findings that ignored problems it was aware of and misrepresented the soundness of the data the company was reporting. It did so in order to please the funder and thereby keep its business. Let us look a bit more closely at why this occurred.

Although the US Securities and Exchange Commission (SEC) requires publicly traded companies to be audited, it allows them to select the auditors and fire them at will (Bazerman and Watkins, 2004: 46). During the 1980s companies approached auditing firms as sophisticated consumers who practiced not only price shopping but also 'opinion shopping', looking for an auditor that would interpret the accounting standards in the way that the company preferred (Boyd, 2004: 380). This put a not-so-subtle pressure on auditors to produce audits that pleased their clients, even if they had to do so at the expense of accurate reports.

The intense competition led to lower profitability for auditing companies (ibid.: 380–1), pushing them to engage in cost-cutting, in part through using low-paid junior staff. Although these junior employees were often unable to advance within the auditing company, they could often gain employment in the client firms (ibid.: 382). Andersen was in no way an exception to this practice and, in fact, went further by actively encouraging these transfers even at senior levels (ibid.: 382–3). Because of this migration there was inevitably a blurring of the lines between auditor and client.

Perhaps even more importantly, the profit squeeze led auditing companies to look for other means of maximizing profits. They found it in consulting services. The share of revenue deriving from audits for the 'Big Six' accounting firms went from 62 per cent in 1982 to just under 50 per cent in 1990 (Jacob, 1991; Boyd, 2004: 384). It is perhaps telling that in 1990 auditing represented a considerably lower than average share of Arthur Andersen's income: under 35 per cent. Management consulting brought in 44 per cent of its revenue. In 1990 Andersen was the only one of the 'Big Six' accounting firms to receive more revenue from management consulting services than it did from auditing (Jacob, 1991; Boyd, 2004: 384).

The decline of the proportion of revenues in auditing firms from actual auditing did not stop in 1990. According to a *Wall Street Journal* article, 75 per cent of the revenue of auditing firms came from non-auditing services in 2001 (Bryan-Low, 2003).

The results of this were inevitable. Auditing considerations were relegated to secondary importance. Although it seems clear that Andersen recognized there were serious issues related to Enron's use of special purpose entities (Toffler, 2003: 211–12; Chandra, 2003: 106; US Senate Committee on Governmental Affairs, 2002: 27–8), Andersen raised no flags about the matter, and the reason for its negligence was likely related to the large amounts of money it received from Enron for consulting as well as auditing. Consider the following passage from a book by a former Andersen employee discussing an internal Andersen memo. The passage clearly suggests that the income Andersen received from Enron was a prime consideration in producing findings about the 'related-party transactions' (involving special purpose entities) that would please Enron:

Andersen proved itself adept at recognizing risk. What the firm didn't know how to do was to stay away from it. 'Ultimately, the conclusion was reached to retain Enron as a client, citing that it appeared we had the appropriate people and processes in place to serve Enron and manage our engagement risks,' the memo read, adding that it was 'not unforeseeable' that fees could reach $100 million a year – a huge amount from any one client... [R]isk assessment and fee generation went hand in hand. Whatever concerns the partners might have had stayed hidden behind the Firm's famous doors. Just one week later, Duncan [one of the partners] met with the audit and compliance committee of Enron's board and told them that the related-party transactions had been 'reviewed for adequacy'. Andersen would be issuing an unqualified audit opinion for the year 2000. (Toffler, 2003: 211–12)

An 'unqualified audit opinion' means that the auditor has examined the reporting of the transactions and found that they are completely acceptable according to accounting standards. The ensuing debacle showed how far from the truth this finding actually was.

While Enron was certainly the most notable scandal, conflict-of-interest issues in auditing investigations of company financial reporting are certainly a more general problem. The possibilities for conflicts of interest were, in fact, noted by Arthur Levitt, former chair of the SEC, who tried unsuccessfully to increase regulation:

> When I was chairman of the Securities and Exchange Commission, we put into place a number of reforms to improve audits and minimize conflicts of interest. But we were largely unsuccessful in persuading accounting firms to separate their auditing businesses from their consulting businesses and in convincing the auditing profession to do a better job of policing itself. (Levitt, 2002)

Increasing economic pressure on accounting firms and the conflicts of interest arising from these pressures may well be the reason for the increase in financial restatements due to accounting inaccuracies between 1997 and 2002. According to a General Accounting Office report, a number of studies indicated that there was an increase in the number of financial restatements in this period. The same report notes that 'Until recently, restatements due to accounting irregularities were seen as primarily affecting small companies and the technology industry. However, for the restatements we identified, the number of large companies restating their financial statements has increased significantly' (US General Accounting Office, 2002: 16). The same study identified 38 per cent of these restatements as involving 'revenue recognition' (ibid.: 19, 21) – that is, restatements that relate to the amount of revenue a company is earning, and thus potentially concerning far more than a mere technical accounting issue.

Although the Sarbanes-Oxley Act in the United States has attempted to address the question of conflict of interest arising from non-auditing activities by auditors, it is unlikely to resolve the issue completely (Boyd, 2004). Nor should this problem be looked at as peculiar to American practices. A 2005 study of accounting practices in the United Kingdom concluded that there was a 'need for continuing attention by regulators worldwide to the enhancement of the integrity of audit and particularly the securing of auditor independence' (Fearnley et al., 2005: 69).

The Enron case shows in a different way from the HRT example how issues of economic self-interest related to funding can affect findings. In the case of Enron, it was not a 'spin' put on the results of investigations but rather the results themselves that were the heart of the misrepresentation. Still, both cases should raise the same cautionary flag. In the critical assessment of research, when the researcher is paid by a party with a large stake in the outcome, the role of the funding in influencing the findings is something that should be considered. As the Enron case shows, the funding in question need not even be for the research itself; it can be just as pernicious when the researcher (in this case the accounting firm) receives money from the interested party for other services. The outcomes of the research, in this case the audits, were seen by the auditor, Andersen, as potentially impacting on non-auditing as well as auditing revenues. This perception made all the difference.

Case 3: *The Bell Curve*

In Cases 1 and 2 we saw how, in two very different fields, the financial interests of the funding sources of research can have a substantial effect on how research is conducted and presented. We also saw that the impact of funding issues can be substantial, affecting our health and our financial well-being.

There are, of course, differences between the two cases. Nevertheless, despite their differences, in both cases the funding may be seen to be directly related to the economic self-interest of the funders or of the researchers themselves. There are situations, however, where the interests of funding bodies or researchers are not financial, but social or political. In critically assessing research we need to be equally aware of such ideological interests.

The Bell Curve: Intelligence and Class Structure in American Life provides an example of how funding can relate directly to social and political interests. Written by noted psychologist Richard J. Herrnstein and Charles Murray, political scientist and fellow at the American Enterprise Institute, *The Bell Curve* exploded on to the American political landscape in 1994. At 845 pages, the book is replete with empirical data presented in the form of graphs, charts and tables. *The Bell Curve* presented statistical data about the heritability of IQ in order to support the thesis that IQ is a predictor of socio-cultural success:

> Matching the status of the groups is usually justified on the grounds that the scores people earn are caused to some extent by their socioeconomic status, so if we want to see the 'real' or 'authentic' difference between them, the contribution of status must be excluded... [S]ocioeconomic status is also a *result* of cognitive ability, as people of high and low cognitive ability move to correspondingly high and low places in the socioeconomic continuum. The reason that parents have high or low socioeconomic status is in part a function of their intelligence, and their intelligence also affects the IQ of their children via both genes and environment. (Herrnstein and Murray, 1994: 286–7)

In this passage Herrnstein and Murray turn on its head the argument that cognitive ability is affected by the social environment. They claim instead that socio-economic status is largely the result, rather than the cause, of differences in IQ.

Despite its length and extensive use of statistical data, *The Bell Curve* drew widespread attention from popular as well as scholarly publications. The book was both heralded and reviled in both types of media. A review in the popular magazine *Forbes* praised it as 'massive, meticulous, minutely detailed, clear', and asserted that its publication was a watershed intellectual event comparable with the publication of Darwin's *Origin of Species* (Brimelow, 1994). Thomas Sowell (1995: 32) in the *American Spectator* praised it as 'very sober, very thorough, and very honest'. Charles Krauthammer (1994) wrote in the *Washington Post* that '*The Bell Curve* is a powerful, scrupulous, landmark study of the relationship between intelligence and social class.' Charles Finn, a former assistant secretary of education in the Reagan administration, wrote in *Commentary*:

> Murray and Herrnstein offer the most extensive documentation to date of these propositions, and their display of the relationship

between intellect and success is the book's most distinctive contribution. The authors also proffer compelling evidence that stratification by intelligence is largely a development of the 20th century, especially of the past several decades, and is fueled by changes in the marriage and labor markets, and above all by the 'sorting' mechanisms of higher education. (Finn, 1995: 80).

However, the popular press did not universally praise *The Bell Curve*. A *New York Times* editorial stated:

> Though 'The Bell Curve' contains serious scholarship, it is also laced with tendentious interpretation. Once unlike-minded scholars have time to react, they will subject its findings to withering criticism. At its best, the Herrnstein-Murray story is an unconvincing reading of murky evidence. At its worst, it is perniciously and purposely incendiary. The graphs, charts, tables and data admit of less dire conclusions. But less dire would not have put Mr. Murray on the cover of news magazines, though it would have given America's disadvantaged a more accurate, hopeful glimpse of their future. (*New York Times*, 1994)

E.J. Dionne (1994) argued:

> The Herrnstein-Murray argument is… not a brave breakthrough but a flashy repackaging of a repeatedly discredited fashion in American life. Whenever we are exhausted with reform, we shrug our shoulders and say, 'there's nothing we can do for that poor guy down the street.' Thus was pseudo-science about racial differences used to justify the end of Reconstruction and the reimposition of a segregated caste system on the American South.

The book incited no less of an incendiary and divided reaction in the scholarly media. In a review of *The Bell Curve* for the journal *Society*, E.L. Pattullo (1996: 86) found that Herrnstein and Murray had demonstrated the book's central thesis – that 'IQ is more closely correlated with social outcomes than is any other factor: negatively with social pathology and positively with social success' – so effectively and definitively 'as to be undeniable'. He went on to state that the book in its entirety reveals its authors to be 'eminently reasonable, responsible, civilized, and compassionate human beings' (ibid.). Pattullo essentially dismissed criticisms of *The Bell Curve* as coming from people with a left-liberal agenda who did not want to face up to the implications of Herrnstein and Murray's arguments for social policy.

In the American Psychological Association journal of book reviews, *Contemporary Psychology*, Thomas J. Bouchard (1995) argued that '*The Bell Curve* carefully documents in table after table, graph after graph that cognitive ability [that is, IQ] has become a more important determinant of social status than social class of origin.' He concluded his review by saying that 'This is a superbly written and exceedingly well documented book. It raises many troubling questions regarding the organization of our society. It deserves the attention of every well informed and thoughtful citizen.'

In the *School Psychology Review*, a journal published by the US National Association of School Psychologists, John Kranzler (1995) wrote that 'Herrnstein and Murray provided considerable empirical support for their detailed arguments in The Bell Curve.' He argued that 'their findings cannot be easily dismissed. Not only did they analyze an excellent set of data with appropriate statistical techniques, but their findings are generally consistent with the results of past studies...'

In the journal *Perspectives on Political Science*, Pat Duffy Hutcheon (1996) wrote:

> By any conceivable criterion, Richard J. Herrnstein and Charles Murray have produced in *The Bell Curve*... an educational work of prodigious scholarship. At the very least their book should be valued as a compendium of vitally important information on what is actually happening to intelligence and class structure in the late twentieth-century United States. For its political significance alone *The Bell Curve* deserves careful perusal and thoughtful assessment.

The criticisms of the book were as harsh as the praise of its supporters was effusive. In the same issue of *Contemporary Psychology* as Bouchard's positive review, Donald Dorfman (1995) wrote '*The Bell Curve* is not a scientific work. It was not written by experts, and it has a specific political agenda.' He stated that 'None of their research analyses on the relation between IQ, SES [socio-economic status], and social behaviors has ever been published in peer reviewed scientific journals' and suggested that one of the authors, Herrnstein, although he was a psychologist, had 'never published any scientific research on the genetic basis of IQ and its relation to race, poverty, or social class in peer reviewed scientific journals in his entire 36 year academic career'. Dorfman pointed out that the second author, Charles Murray, has a degree in political science and also 'has never conducted or published any research in scientific journals on the genetic basis of IQ and poverty in his entire career'.

Ned Block (1995: 99), a professor in the Department of Linguistics and Philosophy at MIT, argued in *Cognition* that '*The Bell Curve*'s main argument for black genetic inferiority in IQ... depends for its persuasive force on conceptual confusions...' In a review for the journal *Psychological Science*, Robert J. Sternberg (1995: 260) observed that '*The Bell Curve* appears not to have been written for scientists, but for laypeople. There is no mention or evidence of genuine peer review, and the book has been marketed primarily through media hype via mass-circulation bookstores. Nor is the book an expansion of a refereed article.' He went on to note that the book makes broad claims, despite a general weakness of the evidence presented in this unrefereed work – a weakness that has not been addressed in the popular media. In a similar attack on the scientific merits of the book, Robert M. Hauser (1995: 149) in *Contemporary Sociology* described it as a 'massive, ideologically driven, and frequently careless or incompetent assemblage of good science, bad science, and pseudo-science that is likely to do great damage both in the realm of public policy and in the conduct of social research'. In another review, Steven A. Gelb (1997: 136) argued 'the book's citation of articles... provided a respectable platform for views not welcomed into the intellectual mainstream of social science discourse since the defeat of nazism'.

Even this cursory summary of the reactions to this controversial book makes clear that one major issue concerning the book's contentions is whether the authors are presenting evidence in a disinterested, scientific manner or whether they are ideologues who are simply searching for evidence to support an ideological agenda. An examination of the funding of one of the authors of the book, as well as the authors of many of the sources to which *The Bell Curve* refers, can help us to understand the context in which it developed. This context is important to determining the degree to which the research can be considered to meet the standards of disinterested scientific inquiry.

According to his biography on the American Enterprise Institute website (American Enterprise Institute, 2009b), Charles Murray, who earned a PhD in political science from MIT, was a resident fellow of the American Enterprise Institute from 1990 until 2003 and is at present a Brady Scholar at the institute. Previous to that he had been a fellow at another research institute, the Manhattan Institute. At both institutes, including the period in which Murray researched and co-authored *The*

Bell Curve, major funding for his positions came from the Bradley Foundation (Kissinger, 1994; DeParle, 1990).

What is noteworthy about all three organizations – the American Enterprise Institute, the Manhattan Institute and the Bradley Foundation – is that they are all generally identified as supporting politically conservative agendas. Let us look at each of these individually.

The American Enterprise Institute (2009a) on its website states:

> From the beginning... the Association's spirit was libertarian and conservative rather than simply 'probusiness.' Its founding mission statement would still serve well: to promote 'greater public knowledge and understanding of the social and economic advantages accruing to the American people through the maintenance of the system of free, competitive enterprise.'

A bit further down the website states: 'The Institute furnishes policymakers with ideas to meet the pressing challenges of today based on the resilient principles of private liberty, individual opportunity, and free enterprise' (ibid.).

These descriptions match the way most American political conservatives describe themselves. The list of scholars and fellows on the American Enterprise Institute website features some of the most prominent contemporary American political conservatives, including David Frum, Lynne Cheney, Newt Gingrich, Irving Kristol, Richard Perle and Paul Wolfowitz. It might be added that the list also includes Charles Murray. Karl Rove (2006), in remarks at the institute, said that 'Our conservative movement is grateful for the intellectual leadership of the American Enterprise Institute.'

The ideological bent of the Manhattan Institute is similarly conservative. Its website boasts that its work 'has won new respect for market-oriented policies and helped make reform a reality' (Manhattan Institute for Policy Research, 2009a). The focus on 'market-oriented policies' is clearly emblematic of a conservative orientation. The Manhattan Institute publishes *City Journal*, a magazine devoted to urban policy issues, which has been credited as being the 'idea factory' for the administration of former New York City mayor Rudolph Giuliani (*City Journal*, undated), a mayor known for conservative policies. The scholars the institute supports also frequently demonstrate a clear conservative ideological bent. Richard Epstein, for example, a Manhattan Institute scholar, wrote a book entitled *Takings: Private Property and the Power of Eminent Domain*, which 'presents a case for sharply rejecting the New Deal state with its expansive powers of taxation and regulation at both the federal and state level' (Manhattan Institute for Policy Research, 2009c). Another Manhattan Institute scholar, Herman Badillo, former New York City congressman, wrote a book entitled *One Nation, One Standard: An Ex-Liberal on How Hispanics Can Succeed Just Like Other Immigrant Groups*. The Manhattan Institute's promotional material for the book describes Badillo as a former believer in the value of government programs to help the Hispanic community, who 'came to see that the real path to prosperity, political unity, and the American mainstream is self-reliance, not big government' (Manhattan Institute for Policy Research, 2009b). In this description we see the use of terms emblematic of an American conservative ideology: 'self-reliance, not big government'.

It is interesting to note that the Manhattan Institute was more skittish than the American Enterprise Institute about insinuating itself into the political maelstrom that *The Bell Curve* might ignite. Around the time that Charles Murray began his collaboration with Richard Herrnstein on *The Bell Curve*, he had been among the best-known scholars at the Manhattan Institute. William Hammett, then president of the Manhattan Institute, said in an interview that he was worried about seeing headlines such as 'White scholar sees genetic inferiority', and both he and Murray agreed that it would be preferable for Murray to leave the institute. Murray moved to the American Enterprise Institute, taking with him an annual grant of approximately $100,000 from the Bradley Foundation (DeParle, 1990).

Not surprisingly the Bradley Foundation, which provided major funding for Murray at both institutes, also has a strong conservative ideological perspective. An article from *Alternatives in Philanthropy*, a publication produced by Capital Research Center, a conservative body focusing on non-profit organizations, stated that 'the Bradley Foundation in 1996 awarded $10.2 million – nearly half of its grants – to prominent conservative policy organizations' (Oliver, 1998). Among the recipients was the American Enterprise Institute.

The Bradley Foundation has had a clear political agenda in giving grants. In discussing the ideological underpinnings of conservative foundations, Michael Joyce, president and CEO of the Bradley Foundation, noted that 'the social problems that consume the interest of grant makers are, at bottom, political; they arise from differences in opinion and interest' (Joyce and Richardson, 1993). The following comments by William Schambra, presently director of the Hudson Institute's Bradley Center and in 1992–1993 director of programs at the

Bradley Foundation (Hudson Institute, 2009), also make clear that the Bradley Foundation provided grants with a clear political agenda in mind:

> Conservative philanthropy understands itself to be engaged in an attempt to scrape away decades of misguided social engineering inflicted on America by its elites. The objective is to restore the original view of constitutional liberal democracy buried beneath a lot of very bad progressive remodeling.
>
> That means that it must fight a pitched political battle against bureaucracies manned by well entrenched professionals, in an attempt to restore the regime of individual rights and local community.
>
> This is how the Bradley Foundation in Milwaukee, where I worked for a while, viewed its grantmaking in the two areas [welfare reform and educational vouchers] where it seems to have had some lasting effect. (Schambra, 2008)

While these remarks do not explicitly relate to *The Bell Curve*, it is certainly worth noting that *The Bell Curve* is concerned with both welfare and education, the two areas alluded to in this selection. In critically assessing this research, it is only prudent to consider the possibility that when the Bradley Foundation provided $800,000 of support to Murray during the eight-year period when he co-authored *The Bell Curve* (Kissinger, 1994), it may also have had an ideological agenda in mind.

However, it is not only the funding of one of the authors of *The Bell Curve* which makes it prudent to consider possible political agendas. There is an interesting relationship between a number of the scholars cited in the book and funding provided by the Pioneer Fund, a non-profit funding organization (Pioneer Fund, undated.a). According to the Pioneer Fund's current president, J. Philippe Rushton, 'it is not altogether surprising that those who oppose *The Bell Curve*'s conclusions attack the Pioneer Fund because *The Bell Curve* cited much research published by Pioneer Fund grantees' (Rushton, 2002: 211). On its website, the Pioneer Fund highlights some of its grantees who have done the most significant and 'celebrated' research. Of the 15 names listed on the website (Pioneer Fund, undated.b), all but three are cited in the bibliography of *The Bell Curve*.

At the time of its initial founding, the purpose of the Pioneer Fund was to support 'research and publicity on topics related to "heredity and eugenics" and "the problems of race betterment"' (Lombardo, 2003: 745). The Pioneer Fund remained faithful to its founding principles. 'For the past fifty or so years, the Pioneer Fund has financed race differences in intelligence... research, which seeks to discover evidence of innate differences in intelligence between the "white" and "black" races' (Jackson, 2006: 17). A significant number of the researchers cited by *The Bell Curve* are thus funded by an organization that has a very clear eugenicist agenda with, at the very least, racialist overtones.

In itself, none of this discredits the claims of the book. There is no evidence that the research findings in *The Bell Curve* were in any way changed to please the conservative funders of one its authors, Charles Murray. However, it is only reasonable to suggest that funding sources do need to be considered in critically assessing this work. Examination of the funding of not only one of the authors but also the sources cited in the work makes it clear that there is at least the possibility that the research findings in *The Bell Curve* were not based on disinterested scientific inquiry, but that, on the contrary, the book was written with a clear political agenda in mind. This in turn would suggest that the research and its findings should be considered at least in part in relation to the battle of political ideologies that concerned the funders and sponsors of one of its authors and a number of the book's sources.

Summary and concluding remarks

As long as researchers need incomes and the research itself requires the purchase of tools and materials, research will require funding sources. There is nothing inherently wrong with this. Funding does not in itself corrupt or taint. That said, we have seen in this chapter that when we critically assess research we should keep in mind the following three points.

- A funding source can use its influence to affect the ways research findings are interpreted.
- Funding can influence research findings.
- The sources of funding may indicate ideological biases.

The first two points relate directly to issues of economic self-interest and conflicts of interest. There is, in fact, institutional awareness that research funding and economic self-interest can be a potent mix. While the financial relationship between research studies and private companies is not always disclosed, academic institutions standardly do have policies requiring that faculty disclose any potential conflicts of interest in their research (Elliott, 2008). Some peer-reviewed periodicals have also instituted conflicts-of-interest policies. An example is *JAMA*, which instituted a policy in 2006 requiring all authors to disclose potential conflicts of interest when they submit a manuscript (Flanagin et al., 2006). This replaces earlier *JAMA* policies that have proven ineffective.

In a similar vein, the American Sarbanes-Oxley Act of 2002 is intended to have a watchdog effect on accounting. The Act is intended to regulate the accounting profession and provide quality control and ethical standards for auditing (Kaplan, 2004: 379–80). Just as disclosure of potential conflicts of interest is intended to prevent such conflicts from corrupting the research process, so Sarbanes-Oxley is intended to provide the ground rules that will prevent auditing companies from being corrupted by the clear financial interest they have in pleasing the corporations that pay them.

These attempts to prevent conflicts of interest from corrupting the research process are important, but are unlikely to forestall altogether the corrupting influences of funding from interested parties (see, for example, Kaplan, 2004; Elliott, 2008). Moreover, the non-expert often learns about research not directly from peer-reviewed journals, but from the mass media, where financial relationships between researchers and industry are not consistently disclosed (see, for example, Hochman et al., 2008). A certain degree of vigilance is therefore likely to be required for the foreseeable future.

The third point we make focuses on ideological rather than economic interests. When we assess research we need to be aware not only of the potential for funding from interested parties to affect the research process, but also the possibility that the funding is indicative of a pre-existing agenda on the part of the researchers. It is relatively easy to understand that when a company funds research on a product it manufactures, it has a clear financial interest in the outcome of that research. When it comes to the research funded by the Bradley Foundation with institutional support from first the Manhattan Institute and then the American Enterprise Institute, however, the interest in the research outcome is not financial but rather political. In such cases the funding from an interested party suggests that the researchers themselves share the agenda of the funding source. As we pointed out earlier, this does not, in itself, mean that the research is not useful. It does mean, however, that we need to look at the research in relation to ideological agendas and search for viewpoints other than those of the researchers to see what might be left out, glossed over or interpreted in particular ways in order to support a specific ideological agenda.

In concluding this chapter, we would like to point out that funding can affect research in even more subtle ways than those we have examined in this chapter. Since research is generally dependent on financial support, what gets funded to some degree determines what gets researched and thus what research questions get asked. Underlying any research question are certain assumptions about the nature of the phenomena being examined. So if certain types of studies are funded while other types are not, certain research questions and accompanying assumptions may become theoretical fixtures because of the selectivity of the funding. In the next chapter we will be looking at research in relation to theoretical frameworks quite independently of funding. Nevertheless, the reader may do well to keep in mind that the issues may be far more interrelated in real life than we can possibly do justice to within the scope of this book.

4

Research paradigms

Introduction

There is a popular image of the independent scholar or scientist happily working away in an office or laboratory, with no other concern than to engage in a relentless pursuit of truth and follow whatever flights of imagination might lead to some revolutionary discovery. Of course, it should come as no great surprise that the reality of how scientists and scholars work is considerably different. Thomas Kuhn (1962), in his seminal account of the history and philosophy of science,[1] describes how the bulk of scientific research unfolds largely within the structure of what he terms 'normal science', and the closely associated concept of 'paradigms'. Paradigms are the system of assumptions and beliefs that are shared by the members of a scientific or scholarly community and guide the research undertaken by the professionals who work within that community.

Scientists and scholars generally do not freely engage in research because a particular question or topic captures their fancy. Rather, they are very seriously engaged in developing solutions to those issues that are recognized as being significant within the paradigm which guides their work. A paradigm adopted by a scholarly or scientific community can exert a fairly rigid control not only over the solutions to problems, but over the problems and questions that scientists can investigate. According to Kuhn (ibid.: 37), 'one of the things a scientific community acquires with a paradigm is a criterion for choosing problems... To a great extent these are the only problems that the community will admit as scientific or encourage its members to undertake.' Normal science is by its very nature conservative: paradigms are not easily disrupted, and scientists in the normal course of their research 'attempt to force nature into the conceptual boxes supplied by professional education' (ibid.: 5), and to resist 'fundamental novelties because they are necessarily subversive of [their] basic commitments' (ibid.).

For the purposes of this book, the important point to bear in mind is that the truth researchers seek to discover is the truth relative to the paradigm in which they operate, and that today's truth may be tomorrow's quaint mythology. Similarly, what is not scientifically 'thinkable' – not a legitimate scientific question within a current paradigm – may be viewed at a later date as a significant breakthrough.

In this chapter, we look at paradigms in three different disciplines. Beginning with psychology, we look at the rise of intelligence testing in the nineteenth century and examine the assumptions about the nature of intelligence that underlie IQ tests. We consider how the dominant paradigm has influenced the problems that researchers in this area investigate. Next we look at the evolving views of medical research about ulcers. We consider the extent to which dominant research paradigms exerted influence over how researchers have viewed this disease and prompted resistance towards an alternative view and treatment. Finally, we turn to literary and fine arts criticism and consider how artistic canons and the assumptions on which they are based can affect what researchers in these fields examine.

Case 1: intelligence testing

The modern history of measuring intelligence may be said to have begun in the nineteenth century with Francis Galton, who argued that it should be possible to assess innate intelligence. For Galton, general intellectual ability was something that was not only biological but also inheritable: 'The direct result of this inquiry,' he wrote in a prefatory chapter to his book *Hereditary Genius*, 'is to make manifest the great and measurable differences between the mental and bodily faculties of individuals and to prove that the laws of heredity are as applicable to the former as to the latter' (Galton, 1962: 35). He investigated the possibility of using eugenics to improve human beings:

> My general object has been to take note of the varied hereditary faculties of men, and of the great differences in different families and races, to learn how far history may have shown the practicability of supplanting inefficient human stock by better strains, and to consider whether it might not be our duty to do so by such efforts as may be reasonable... (Galton, 1907: 1)

The measures Galton developed were not actually useful (Fancher, 1985: 80; Richardson and Bynner, 1984: 505). However, Alfred Binet, in collaboration with Victor Henri and Theodore Simon, did develop puzzle-type tests for measuring cognitive abilities that could be used to predict educational success, and in particular to differentiate between those who would not learn from those who could not (Thorndike, 1997: 5; Ittenbach et al., 1997: 21) – in other words, to differentiate those who were genetically capable but unwilling to learn from those who lacked the innate intellectual capacity to do so.

Charles Spearman refined the tests by focusing on their reliability. As part of that refinement, Spearman (1904) introduced the idea of 'general intelligence', a single, unitary faculty, which he saw as underlying the ability to perform specific cognitive operations. He believed that this general intelligence was innate: 'the correspondence selected for inquiry in the present case is that between *natural innate faculties*. By this definition, we explicitly declare that all such individual circumstances as after birth materially modify the investigated function are irrelevant and must be adequately eliminated...' (ibid.: 227). He believed that this correspondence between natural innate faculties was to a great extent an inheritable, physiological property, and hoped, just as Galton had, that it could be used for eugenic social purposes (Fancher, 1985: 95).

The same emphasis on intelligence as a unitary inheritable quality is found in the work of later developers of intelligence testing, such as Henry Herbert Goddard and Robert Yerkes and his colleague Robert Brigham. Yerkes and Brigham were able to give their intelligence tests on a large scale to US soldiers during the First World War. Their results showed that certain groups – European immigrants, particularly those from southern and eastern Europe – scored significantly lower than native-born white Americans, and that African Americans scored below these groups. Brigham especially argued that these differences were racial and genetic in nature (ibid.: 127–30).

Lewis Terman, who in refining the Binet-Simon test created the Stanford-Binet test widely used in schools, also believed that what was at issue were innate differences in ability. He believed that distinguishing between those who had ability and those who did not would improve pedagogy (Thorndike, 1997: 9).

The advent of widespread IQ testing in the 1920s may well have been the result of this conception of intelligence becoming dominant in the United States: 'Tests were seen as measuring innate talent and as providing a way to solve society's problems' (ibid.: 10). The growth of IQ testing in the United States continued for nearly half a century (ibid.:

11–12; Fass, 1980): 'The period from the 1920s to the 1960s saw an explosion in the use of tests in every phase of American life. Group tests of intelligence became common in the schools and the growing field of clinical psychology… began applying measures of intellect to adults in various civilian contexts outside of education' (Thorndike, 1997: 12).

The extensive use of IQ tests was not restricted to the United States. They were also widely used in education in mid-twentieth-century Britain for similar reasons (Chan and East, 2004, 2008: 8). The '11-plus' examination which included an IQ test was administered to children around 11 years of age and determined the kind of education they would receive:

> The child's score on this examination largely determines which type of secondary school he will attend. The students acquiring the highest scores attend grammar schools. However, they may choose to attend a technical school. The remainder, constituting roughly 60 to 75 per cent of the total age group, attend secondary modern schools. The I.Q. cutting point for grammar schools varies from district to district, but seldom falls below 110, and is usually between 114 and 120. (Montague, 1959: 375)

Throughout much of the twentieth century, the theoretical view that IQ tests measure a unitary and inheritable physical capacity continued to be well entrenched as the dominant paradigm. Perhaps the most notable proponents were Cyril Burt, Arthur Jensen and the authors of *The Bell Curve*, Richard Herrnstein and Charles Murray.

Burt's research began in the early twentieth century and continued through the 1970s. He first focused on a study of the IQs of two groups of British students: one group from a normal elementary school and the other from an exclusive preparatory school. He concluded that the differences in IQ between the groups related to inheritance. Later, Burt conducted studies purportedly using identical twins separated at birth in order to provide incontrovertible proof of the heritability of IQ. However, researchers in the late 1970s discovered that his research on this topic was fraudulent (Fancher, 1985: 200–25).

Arthur Jensen, an American psychologist, promoted explicitly racialist views in his famous 1969 article, 'How much can we boost IQ and scholastic achievement?' Using Burt's conception of intelligence as an inherited trait, Jensen (1969: 82) argued with respect to the lower IQ scores of African Americans that 'The preponderance of the evidence is, in my opinion, less consistent with a strictly environmental hypothesis than with a genetic hypothesis, which, of course, does not exclude the influence of environment or its interaction with genetic factors.'

A similar theoretical paradigm informed the work of Herrnstein and Murray in *The Bell Curve*. Here too the intelligence tests were looked at as measuring at least to a considerable degree a unitary, inheritable, physical trait. Among the conclusions that Herrnstein and Murray (1994: 22–3) consider to be 'beyond significant technical dispute' were the following: 'There is such a thing as a general factor of cognitive ability on which human beings differ' and 'Cognitive ability is substantially heritable, apparently no less than 40 percent and no more than 80 percent.'

However, not all psychologists accepted the unitary nature of intelligence or the idea that it is to a great extent an inheritable quality. Alfred Binet, for one, was skeptical about the ability of the tests to measure intelligence, if for no other reason than he did not believe it was something that could be measured in a linear, unitary manner. In discussing the test he devised he wrote, 'This scale properly speaking does not permit the measure of the intelligence, because intellectual qualities are not superposable, and therefore cannot be measured as linear surfaces are measured, but are on the contrary, a classification, a hierarchy among diverse intelligences; and for the necessities of practice this classification is equivalent to a measure' (Binet, 1916: 40–1). In other words, Binet looked at his cognitive tests as an empirical way of identifying the class of intelligence to which an individual belonged (the class of those unable to learn, for example) rather than as a way of ranking individuals on a linear scale in relation to their intellectual ability.

In contrast to Spearman's theory of a unitary general intelligence, E.L. Thorndike believed that intelligence was multifaceted and could not be reduced to a single construct. 'The primary fact,' he wrote, 'is that intelligence is not one thing but many' (Thorndike, 1920: 287). In addition, while acceding to the notion that there are certain factors of intelligence that 'might in original nature be absorbed into one unitary ability to learn', Thorndike (1921: 151) downplayed the role of inheritance in accounting for the complex nature of intelligence. He argued that 'many of the complexities of individual differences are superadded by likenesses and differences in training', and concluded the argument by saying that 'even if we did dissect out all the consequences of nurture, leaving only a skeleton of inborn capacities, the organization of these would still be much more complex than that required by Spearman's theory' (ibid.).

Other psychologists identified specific kinds of intelligence. L.L. Thurstone, for example, identified seven clusters of 'Primary Mental Abilities', consisting of 'Verbal Comprehension, Word Fluency, Number Facility, Spatial Visualization, Associative Memory, Perceptual Speed, and Reasoning' (Fancher, 1985: 160). Each one of these represented a 'largely independent element of the intellect' (ibid.). J.P. Guilford posited 120 different categories of intellectual activity, arguing that the intellect is 'much too complex to be subsumed by a few primary mental abilities, much less by a single *g*-factor value or IQ score' (ibid.). For psychologist Howard Gardner, Thurstone's and Guilford's critiques of the concept of a unitary intelligence do not go far enough. For him, intelligence cannot be encapsulated by a score on a test. Gardner (1993) formulated the notion of 'multiple intelligences', which refers to the range of skills and abilities people develop in order to adapt to and navigate the demands of their way of life. For Gardner, whatever is innate in intellectual capacity is developed through education: 'intelligences, to a great extent, are shaped by cultural influences and refined by educational processes. Although all humans exhibit the range of intelligences, individuals differ – presumably both for hereditary and environmental reasons – in the extent to which these intelligences are developed in various settings' (Chen and Gardner, 1997: 107).

Still, despite the fact that the unitary, heritable model of intelligence was not universally accepted, it remained the dominant paradigm. There is nothing in and of itself wrong with this. In fact, in most fields of inquiry one or another paradigm becomes dominant for a period of time, resists challenges, but then eventually is replaced by another paradigm (Kuhn, 1962). That said, it is worth noting that a dominant paradigm may lead us to accept less critically research that seems to support it than research that conflicts with it. The significance attributed to Cyril Burt's study of separated twins provides a good example of how research may not be thoroughly subjected to the rigors of scientific scrutiny when its conclusions support and confirm the dominant research paradigm.

Burt's research was praised lavishly by reputable scientists, including William Shockley, a Nobel laureate in physics (Tucker, 1994: 338). The study was purported to be the closest thing to proof positive of the hereditary nature of intelligence, since similarities in the IQs of separated twins could not be attributed to their having been raised in similar environments. The noted British psychologist Hans Eysenck called Burt's study the '*only* one of its kind in which the calculation of heritability had any meaning' (ibid.). Nevertheless, for many years detailed information about Burt's twin study was lacking:

[Burt] had never presented detailed case studies of his subjects, as other investigators... had... When other psychologists wrote to Burt asking for his raw data, they were usually politely but effectively put off with references to obscure documents from the 1910s and 1920s, or excuses regarding the unavailability or uncodability of data. Finally, when the American sociologist Christopher Jenks requested simply a list of the fifty-three pairs of IQ scores, and the occupational ratings for the adoptive parents, Burt provided this bare-bones information – but only after a delay of several weeks. This represented the maximum detail with which he ever described his basic data. (Fancher, 1985: 183–4)

On the other hand, Leon Kamin's research on Burt's work encountered difficulties because it criticized Burt's research – research that supported the dominant paradigm. Kamin (1974: 35–47) reviewed Burt's study and demonstrated that it was riddled with inconsistencies, internal contradictions and imprecise data collection (see also Block and Dworkin, 1974b: 55). Kamin presented the results of his analysis of Burt's study in an invited talk at the conference of the Eastern Psychological Association in 1973 (Tucker, 1994: 340). The address was sufficiently well received that Kamin was contacted by Harvard University Press, which sought to publish a book-length version of it. However, the anonymous reviewers who evaluated the manuscript that Kamin submitted recommended against publication. Kamin was later informed that his manuscript had been circulated around Harvard to the very scientists whose work he opposed (ibid.). They were 'blocking the publication of Kamin's work at the same time that they were coordinating a response to it' (ibid.). Nevertheless, it turned out that Kamin's criticisms were on target. Moreover, as noted above, Burt's research findings were found to be fraudulent as well (Fancher, 1985: 200–25).

Such reactions are, at least to some extent, to be expected. Those who support an idea are likely to look favorably at research which confirms their opinions and more critically at research which does not. The dominant paradigm about intelligence has touched on a number of sensitive political and moral issues, and so one would expect strong reactions. Still, it is important for us to keep in mind that work supporting the dominant paradigm may be looked on more favorably and with a less critical eye than work which questions that research.

Perhaps, though, the most important effect of a dominant paradigm such as the unitary, heritable model of intelligence is not how it impacts on research that tends to support or to conflict with it, but rather on how it shapes assumptions and research questions of all research on the topic. Let us look for a moment once again at what Chen and Gardner (1997) say in articulating Gardner's theory of multiple intelligences: 'intelligences, to a great extent, are shaped by cultural influences and refined by educational processes' (see also Gardner, 1993). Gardner rejects the notion that there is a unitary factor that constitutes intelligence. He also appears to reject the view that intelligences are primarily innate. Still, he does accept the basic terms of the debate as framed within the dominant theoretical paradigm. That is, he accepts the theoretical assumption that it is possible to make some kind of distinction between cultural influences and the raw material that is being shaped.

This dichotomy is, in fact, the core of the nature versus nurture debate. However, it is not at all clear that the dichotomy is necessary. Key to the nature-nurture dichotomy is the assumption that a genetic trait is expressed to some degree independently of the environment. However, in many instances if an environment changes, the trait under consideration can disappear. Consider, for example, phenylketonuria (PKU), a genetic disorder caused by a recessive gene. Mental retardation occurs if the infant ingests a chemical (phenylalanine) that is found in normal diets. Nevertheless, if this chemical is removed from the diet, the retardation is reduced or even eliminated. The gene is the same, but its interaction with the environment leads to a different expression (Sternberg et al., 2005: 54).

One could study intelligence from such a perspective, looking at the mechanism of how environment and genetics interact to produce intellectual capabilities. Such studies, however, are not what a nature versus nurture framework encourages: the focus of this framework is on the debate about the relative contributions of nature versus the environment to intellectual capacity, rather than on the interactions between the two. When one looks at research results, it is important to remember that the outcomes are in part a function of what questions are being asked: different questions may result in entirely different kinds of outcomes. Here again the point is not to suggest to the reader that we should not take seriously research findings, but rather to suggest that we should recognize the dependence of research findings on particular theoretical frameworks or paradigms. Conclusions that seem to be obviously true within a particular paradigm may seem less obvious when the same phenomena are viewed through the lens of an alternative theoretical framework.

Case 2: what causes ulcers?

Stomach troubles, dyspepsia, ulcers. Whatever name is used, human beings have long been concerned with stomach ailments. However, the medical history of the ulcer really begins in the nineteenth century with an English doctor, William Brinton. In a research article, Brinton noted that there were stomach ulcers in 2–13 per cent of the bodies on which he and others had performed autopsies (Grob, 2003: 551). The discovery that barium could be used to study both the esophagus and the stomach led to radiology becoming the prime means of diagnosing stomach ulcers in living human beings until the 1930s. It was at this point supplemented by endoscopy, which allowed doctors to look directly into the stomach and esophagus (ibid.: 552).

As a result of the new-found ability to identify ulcers first and foremost as a distinct category of ailment, an increasing number of people were identified as suffering from the ailment. Even in the early twentieth century there was certainly some awareness that the increased number of diagnoses may have been related to the new diagnostic techniques. Consider the following comment about one type of peptic ulcers, duodenal, in a 1916 volume of the *New York Medical Journal*: 'Duodenal ulcer either is becoming more frequent or our means of diagnosis more accurate' (Austin, 1916: 984).

Whether the actual incidence of peptic ulcers was increasing or they were simply being diagnosed more frequently may not be known. What is clear is that there appeared to be an increase. Certainly, the reported incidence of death from ulcers significantly increased from the beginning to the middle of the twentieth century. From 1900 to 1943 the death rate that was reported to be due to peptic ulcers rose from 2.8 per thousand in 1900 to 6.8 per thousand in 1943 (Grob, 2003: 552).

Not surprisingly under these circumstances, peptic ulcer became an object of widespread research interest. In 1946 the American Gastroenterological Society identified over 700 research projects that focused on peptic ulcers (ibid.).

What caused peptic ulcers was, however, less clear than their increasing prominence. Gastric acids were clearly identified as part of the problem. Trying to nullify these acids was a form of treatment that was developed at the beginning of the twentieth century and still continues to be used. However, since everyone has gastric acids, the real question was why these acids sometimes caused ulcers and other times did not. One hypothesis proposed quite early on in the twentieth century was that the problem was caused by germs. There was, however, no evidence to support this theory, and although it had many supporters initially, the inability to demonstrate that infections, excessive acidity and ulcers were related may have led to the germ hypothesis falling out of favor by the 1930s (ibid.: 558).

At the same time, there was increasing interest in psychosomatic explanations. Researchers found that stress could increase the secretion of gastric acids, and the idea that stress was a key component in the disease gained widespread acceptance by the middle of the century (ibid.: 558–62). A discussion of the treatment for ulcer patients written by a gastroenterologist and published in the 1952 volume of the *American Journal of Nursing* provides a good illustration of the thinking at the time. Although the author argues that it is not clear if psychotherapy will help, he makes it clear that the emotional component is likely to be an important factor:

> Despite the fact that the exact cause of peptic ulcers is not known, much has been learned about the disordered function of the digestive tract that is associated with ulcer formation, and the personality problems of patients who develop ulcers. Most investigators favor the view that there are multiple factors of importance in the pathogenesis of ulcers. There is a growing conviction that peptic ulcer develops as a result of disturbed function of the stomach which stems from a basic emotional disorder. If this is true, psychiatric treatment would be the most rational, and perhaps the most effective, approach. While increasing attention is being paid to the emotional aspects of this disease, specific knowledge of the psychogenic factors and their control has not advanced sufficiently for a definitive evaluation of the effectiveness of psychotherapeutic measures. (Cassel, 1952: 852)

Hospitalization was recommended for the initial treatment, not only for medical reasons but also because 'moving a patient from his environment often liberates him from actual or fantasied sources of emotional stress' (ibid.: 853). Sedatives such as Phenobarbital were proposed as a way of relieving tension (ibid.).

The idea of stress as a major factor in ulcers was hardly a flash in the pan. In his influential book *The Stress of Life*, originally published in 1956, Hans Selye provided 'reams of experimental justification for stress as the ultimate cause of peptic ulcers' (Spiro, 1998). His revised edition of the book published in 1976 still made the same basic claim: 'It is...

common knowledge that *gastric and duodenal ulcers* are most likely to occur in people who are somewhat maladjusted to their work or family life and suffer from tension and frustration' (Selye, 1976: 259–60). He proposed a mechanism to account for the role stress plays in the development of ulcers: 'Apparently in man chronic gastric ulcers, which normally are well under control, also perforate during stress, because an excess of anti-inflammatory stimuli breaks down the resistance of the barricade' (ibid.: 262).

Nevertheless, the stress paradigm proved wrong. It was not just that a particular hypothesis positing stress as the main causal factor proved incorrect. It turned out that there was another simpler way of looking at peptic ulcers: as the result of bacterial infection rather than the product of psychosomatic stress. In 1982 two Australian physicians, Robbin Warren and Barry Marshall, identified a bacterium, *Helicobacter pylori* (*H. pylori*), in inflamed stomachs but not in normal ones (Atwood, 2004). At first the connection they posited between the presence of the bacteria and ulcers was quite tentative: 'If these bacteria are truly associated with gastritis... they may have a part to play in other poorly understood, gastritis associated diseases (i.e., peptic ulcer and gastric cancer)' (Warren and Marshall, 1983, quoted in Atwood, 2004). It should be pointed out that this hypothesis did not result from an isolated flash of brilliance at a time when no one else was looking at these bacteria in relation to ulcers. To the contrary, there were other investigations and even publications that hinted at a possible relation (Christie and Tansey, 2002: 99). Nevertheless, Marshall in particular did push the hypothesis forward and in collaboration with other researchers published a paper arguing that there was solid evidence linking the *H. pylori* bacterium with ulcers (ibid.: 102).

Warren and Marshall's work did lead to a burst of activity in investigating the infectious disease paradigm for ulcers (Atwood, 2004). This is not to say that the new paradigm was quickly accepted by the medical community (US Centers for Disease Control and Prevention, 2006). That acceptance took well over a decade to occur. While it would be incorrect to say that the bacterial infection paradigm was blocked by a massive conspiracy within the pharmacological industry or the medical profession (Atwood, 2004; Christie and Tansey, 2002: 93–102), it was nevertheless only in 1994 that a National Institutes of Health Consensus Development Conference decided that there was a link between *H. pylori* and peptic ulcers, and it was not until 1996 that the US Food and Drug Administration (FDA) approved antibiotic treatment (US Centers for Disease Control and Prevention, 2006).

Why the delays? Three factors seem to have been at play. First, the scientific and medical community are inherently cautious and skeptical (Atwood, 2004). As we noted in the introduction to this chapter, this conservatism is characteristic of normal science (Kuhn, 1962). Perhaps as a result of this conservative attitude, Marshall, for one, was viewed at times as a fanatic. A scientist involved in ulcer research recalls: 'In the late 1980s I went off to talk around Australia about antisecretory drugs. I went there thinking, "Here I am, talking about acid, and this is Australia's own germ". I mentioned Barry Marshall, and there were hollow laughs from all the gastroenterologists. He was widely disliked at that stage, because he was such an evangelist for the germ' (Roy Pounder in Christie and Tansey, 2002: 93).

The second reason for the delays would appear to be that there was no new drug involved, so the pharmacological industry did not have a material interest in pushing for acceptance. In fact, the industry was making money because the antacids often had to be used on a chronic basis (ibid.: 93–5). So ideological conservatism in this case dovetailed nicely with economic self-interest.

Finally, solid evidence takes time to be developed, and it was not at all clear that the new theory meant to any degree an actual advance in treatment. Doctors were able to use antacids to treat ulcers quite effectively. The real advantage to antibiotic treatment was not so much that it was more effective in treating ulcers but that it was far more effective in preventing their reoccurrence, and this took time to demonstrate (Atwood, 2004). This may explain why it took so long for the information to filter down to practitioners. Indeed, both primary-care physicians and gastroenterologists were slow to respond to the latest treatment recommendations. In 1994 the National Institutes of Health recommended that ulcer patients be treated with antibiotics (US Centers for Disease Control and Prevention, 2006). Nevertheless, national surveys conducted in 1994 and 1996 showed that while 90 per cent of both primary-care physicians and gastroenterologists recognized *H. pylori* as the primary cause of ulcers, 'primary-care physicians reported treating approximately 50% of patients with first-time ulcer symptoms with antisecretory agents *without testing for H. pylori*; in comparison, gastroenterologists reported treating approximately 30% of patients with first-time ulcer symptoms with these agents' (US Centers for Disease Control and Prevention, 1997, emphasis added). Physicians who have not seen for themselves that a treatment makes any difference are not likely to adopt it, no matter what the research shows.

As slow as the scientific and medical communities were in accepting the new paradigm, it was even more difficult for the general public. At least one survey indicated that in 1995 72 per cent of Americans did not know there was an association between *H. pylori* and peptic ulcers (ibid.). A 1997 study taken after the FDA approved antibiotic treatment for ulcers indicated that the situation had not changed: only 27 per cent of the public were aware of the relationship (ibid.). Indeed, the survey showed that 60 per cent continued to believe that ulcers were caused by too much stress (ibid.). For several decades, in fact, the prevalence of peptic ulcers was viewed as rooted in the lifestyles of patients: stress and diet. Indeed, a peptic ulcer was considered to be a 'badge of success', an emblem of the status of the driven professional (Rogers, 1997).

So, what can we learn from the different ways of viewing and treating ulcers? The most appropriate watchword is perhaps caution, in particular caution about embracing a dominant theoretical framework and assuming that the answers to pressing problems will necessarily be solved within it.

The resistance to modifying long-held beliefs that are fundamental within dominant research paradigms represents a reluctance to change that is perhaps characteristic of human beings. It also represents a cautious skepticism towards the wholesale adoption of a new paradigm in the absence of convincing proof that the old paradigm is inadequate and the new one is superior (see Atwood, 2004).

This may be just as true for the present germ theory as it was for the stress theory that it replaced. Indeed, the reality is considerably more complex than the present paradigm would suggest, and includes anomalies for which we do not at this point have an explanation. One major problematic fact is that most people infected with *H. pylori* do not develop ulcers (Rogers, 1997: 4). And, while it is indeed true that eradicating *H. pylori* both cures the infection and reduces the likelihood of its recurrence (ibid.; Hogue, 2008: 862), it is curious that the incidence of peptic ulcers has remained constant in the United States since the mid-1990s, despite the fact that treatment of the *H. pylori* infection is now widespread. The constant rate of peptic ulcers also holds in Asian countries, although *H. pylori* infection is more prevalent there than in the United States (ibid.: 863). To complicate matters further, although *H. pylori* has been prevalent in humans for thousands of years (Ahmed, 2005), the prevalence of ulcers has seen considerable ebbs and flows (Michael Langman in Christie and Tansey, 2002: 25). Moreover, there is evidence that *H. pylori* has beneficial effects and that its absence may be associated with certain types of gastric cancer (Ahmed, 2005).

What is more, while the relationship between *H. pylori* and ulcers is well established, the role of stress, though not causative as had been believed for decades, cannot be eliminated. A small, randomized study of the use of stress management for peptic ulcers in Korea 'demonstrated a significant improvement in both symptoms and ulcer healing' (Hogue, 2008: 863). Environmental factors such as stress, diet, smoking and so on may be implicated in why some people who are infected with *H. pylori* develop ulcers while others do not (see the discussions in Christie and Tansey, 2002).

Will the dominant infection paradigm for ulcers be the one that allows researchers to account for these issues? In examining intelligence tests we saw that at times a paradigm may stop us from thinking about issues that another paradigm may bring to the forefront. Thus even when we can identify problems within a paradigm, we may not be able to solve them within it. The problem of reoccurrence of ulcers was quite clear within the stress paradigm. The paradigm, however, did not provide the best means of addressing the issue. Moreover, given that there are still many issues that have not been solved within the infection paradigm, it would be foolish to assume that this will necessarily be the framework within which future advances will be made. Nor can we assume that a new theoretical framework will not meet the same kind of resistance that met the infection paradigm when it was introduced.

Case 3: artistic canons

We have seen how a dominant theory can prevent researchers from articulating problems, and how even when it can allow for the articulation of a problem, it may not be the framework that allows us to solve it. Here we look at another way in which a theoretical framework can affect research: the way in which it can lead to some subjects being considered worthy and others unworthy of investigation.

Within the arts there are works that are generally considered classics, be it in literature, music or the fine arts. These are the works that are primarily studied in schools and from which younger artists learn their craft. These works may be considered an artistic canon.

An artistic canon, however, is not something that appears from nowhere. It is, by definition, a selection made by human beings from the corpus of artistic works available to them. Moreover, since it is always intended to be a selection of the best and/or the most significant works of this corpus, the selection is based in one way or another on a theory of what about an artistic work gives it aesthetic merit or significance. Given this, it is not surprising that in different cultures and different eras, canons can consist of very different works.

There is often no one person or work that establishes an artistic canon. It is often simply the general consensus by specialists of what is good and/or significant. Nevertheless, this consensus can often be based on unspoken political and cultural assumptions about the worthiness of works from particular groups of people. And this in turn can affect in significant ways what researchers investigate and write about. Below we will look briefly at mid-twentieth-century canons in literature and fine arts, and then examine what they excluded, how they have been changed as a result of challenges and how this has in turn affected the topics that researchers research.

Let us look at the *Norton Anthology of English Literature*. The literary selections in the *Norton Anthology*, which appears as a new edition about every six years, represent the canon of English literature and are an important tool in the acculturation of literature students into the current literary aesthetic. Since its inception in 1962 the *Norton Anthology* has been the premier college textbook of English literature (Donadio, 2006). In fact, it is widely recognized as *the* authoritative encapsulation of the canon. *The Harvard Crimson* describes it as 'the preeminent collection of the English canon', and notes that 'what is included in the anthology influences what is studied in English-literature courses across America and around the world' (Beckett, 2006). Similarly, Rachel Donadio (2006), in an essay in the *New York Times Book Review*, describes the *Norton Anthology* as the 'sine qua non of college textbooks, setting the agenda for the study of English literature in this country and beyond', and notes that its editor is 'symbolically seen as arbiter of the canon'. In considering the changes that have taken place in the *Norton Anthology* over time, Stephen Greenblatt, who took over the reins as general editor in 2006 from the original editor M.H. Abrams, showed his recognition of the intimate relationship between changes in the canon and changes in the *Anthology*: 'The 20th century is of course where you'd expect most of the changes to be, because significant writers keep coming, but already in the seventh edition and continuing into the eighth, a different conception of the shape of the canon has been emerging' (Gewertz, 2006).

The process by which literary works are selected for the *Norton Anthology of English Literature* is indicative of how canons are formed. 'To update each new edition... the editors consulted reader surveys distributed to several hundred professors, who checked off which works they taught most often' (Donadio, 2006). In this way the *Norton Anthology* reflected the canon as it is perceived by the professoriate that transmits it to the next generation.

The 1999 edition marked the first significant shift in the interpretation of the canon. According to Julia Reidhead, a Norton vice-president and editor, changing tastes in the classroom resulted in Norton expanding the canon to include more women and post-colonial writers (ibid.). Each edition since has incorporated additional changes.

It is illustrative to compare the tables of contents of the first 1962 edition with the eighth edition of 2006. In volume 2 of the 1962 edition, which covers the Romantic period (1798–1832) to the mid-twentieth century, the authors are all from the British Isles and almost entirely male. A volume of over 1,600 pages includes the works of only five women (Elizabeth Barrett Browning, Emily Brontë, Christina Rossetti, Katherine Mansfield and Virginia Woolf – see www.wwnorton. com/college/english/nael/noa/pdf/TOC_NAEL1_vol_2.pdf).

Volume 2 of the 2006 edition is considerably longer than its 1962 counterpart, and there is a marked contrast in the kinds of writers included. Twenty-seven different female authors are represented. Moreover, the writers included do not just hail from the British Isles; its scope has been widened to include writers from the Commonwealth nations as well – there is, for example, representation from the Caribbean, Kenya, Nigeria, South Africa and India. By means of the works selected, moreover, the 2006 edition recognizes the significance of the political context within which literature is created, and implicitly attributes value to literary works that are explicitly political. There is, for example, a section entitled 'The "Woman Question": The Victorian Debate about Gender'. Also included is Mina Loy's 'Feminist Manifesto'. There is a section entitled 'Nation and Language', which includes 'Colonization in Reverse' by the Jamaican writer Louise Bennett and 'Decolonizing the Mind' by the Kenyan writer Ngũgĩ Wa Thiong'o. Works from two politically engaged South African writers, Nadine Gordimer and J.M. Coetzee, are also included. The fact that works of a frankly political nature were selected for inclusion in the eighth edition of the prestigious *Norton Anthology* again stands in marked contrast to the 1962 edition, which included far fewer works dealing with issues of current political controversy (see http://media.wwnorton.com/cms/contents/nael_volume2.pdf).

Although the *Norton Anthology of English Literature* gradually moved towards greater inclusiveness, it was not representative of all literatures written in English. Norton did not recognize American literature as significant enough to be anthologized until 1979. The first edition of the *Norton Anthology of American Literature* appeared following the major canon debates of the 1960s and 1970s. Now in its seventh edition (2007), it is reflective of the changes that have taken place in the canon, both in the diversity of the ethnic origins of the writers it includes and in the variety of the kinds of works covered. It now includes writings of Native Americans, the work of the one-time slave, abolitionist and suffragist Frederick Douglass, twentieth-century African American writers, a wide representation of women writers and Asian American writers as well. There is also an excerpt from Art Spiegelman's *Maus: A Survivor's Tale*, a novel written in comic-book format, in which the author recounts his father's experiences during the Nazi Holocaust (see http://media.wwnorton.com/cms/contents/ naal7_toc_complete.pdf).

What led to these changes in the literary canon? The upheavals of the late 1960s in the United States are often considered to be the stimulus. The first black studies program in the United States was instituted at San Francisco State University in 1968 (Colon, 2003) in response to student unrest, and was soon followed by the establishment of black studies courses and programs at other universities for similar reasons (*Time*, 1970; Alkalimat, 1986: 15–16). Soon after, in 1970, the first women's studies department was founded at San Diego State College (San Diego State University, 2006). In both cases what followed the institutionalization of these studies was a growth in the creation of journals focused on these areas (Alkalimat, 1986: 6–7; see also *Ulrichsweb.com*) and at the very least a higher profile and a somewhat greater acceptance of artistic and intellectual work from these groups – if for no other reason than works by women and African Americans were now a standard part of university curricula.

Cause and effect are difficult to determine in analyzing social change. Still, there is no doubt that the institutionalization of such programs and in more general terms the greater acceptance of writings from authors in these groups led to the shift in the *Norton Anthology* selections discussed above. Presumably these were also considerations for Norton when it began to publish anthologies of women's and African American literature – another indication of the growing acceptability of work previously ignored.

The literary canon can affect substantially what researchers research in literature. In the early twentieth century, for example, when American literature was not an accepted part of the literary canon even in the

United States, F.O. Matthieson, who was to be become a famous literary critic, did not even begin to read the literature of his own country until after he received his BA from Yale. He then became interested in Walt Whitman and wanted to write his doctoral dissertation on him at Harvard, but 'was persuaded by his professors to write on something more significant: Elizabethan translation' (Levine, 1996: 83–4). Now that the canon has changed to accept American literature and to look at Whitman as a great American poet, it is rather unlikely that a doctoral student would be pressured to write on another subject for these reasons.

However, it is not only external pressure that is at issue. If certain writers or works are not deemed to be important then it is unlikely that researchers will even have a desire to write about them. One literary scholar, for example, has noted that although her field of study is nineteenth-century American literature, for a long time she did not read James Fenimore Cooper because of the negative way in which he was viewed in the academy, and was amazed to find him a highly accomplished writer when she finally did happen to read his works (ibid.: 91–2).

The questioning of the literary canon that began during the late 1960s and continued for over two decades has wrought immense changes in what is being researched. To get a sense of the difference, consider this comparison of the 1958 and 1982 Modern Language Association annual meetings:

> In 1958, as I need hardly report, none of the papers or sessions was devoted to the work of a black writer – much less of a Native American, Asian American, or other 'ethnic' writer. There was, of course, a session devoted to Spanish-American Literature; characteristically, the papers concerned subjects like the second phase of modernismo in Chile and German literature in Mexican periodicals of the late nineteenth century. A discussion group for thirty-five people treated the new subject of Hispanic area studies, but nothing in the program suggested a concern for the writings of Chicanos or Puerto Ricans. Nor was there much interest in the writing of women. (Lauter, 1991: 5)

On the other hand, the 1982 convention showed a 'striking increase in the proportion of white women and minority professors on the program and the equally apparent increase of papers devoted to the work of minority and white women authors' (ibid.: 6–7).

This is not to suggest that everyone believes these changes have been for the better. Harold Bloom (1994), for one, has argued notably that the shifts in the literary canon have had a deleterious effect on academic practice and intellectual thought. Our point here, however, is not to argue the pros and cons of shifts in the canon, but merely to point out that the literary canon – that is, what are considered to be important or significant literary works – does change and has an effect on what is researched that should not be ignored.

Although perhaps less prominent in both academia and the general public, the same kind of exclusivity that has marked the literary canon has also been characteristic of the canon in the visual arts. The canonical tradition in art, like its counterpart in other disciplines, encapsulates a conception of what it means to be a great artist in that field.

Like the literary canon, the traditional fine arts canon is composed of Western white men. This point is illustrated by a book entitled *The Metropolitan Museum of Art* (Hibbard, 1980), which reviews the holdings of the New York museum of the same name. Although there are special sections devoted to such subjects as Egypt, the Ancient Near East, Islamic art and Far Eastern art, the bulk of the volume is divided into chronological periods, and the artists covered in these sections are Western and overwhelmingly male.

The canon in the visual arts has tended to be even more impervious to the inclusion of women and black artists than the literary canon. Nevertheless, here too social activism, especially among American women and to a lesser extent African Americans, has led to the canon being questioned and, as a consequence, research on previously ignored artists. Although much of the debate about the literary canon has focused on the exclusion of literature written by both women and African American writers, feminist critiques of the fine arts canon appear to be more pervasive than African American critiques.[2] For this reason, our focus here is on female visual artists and the canon.

Linda Nochlin, among the earliest of feminist art critics, compares women's participation in literature with their participation in art:

> While art making traditionally has demanded the learning of specific techniques and skills, in a certain sequence, in an institutional setting outside the home, as well as becoming familiar with a specific vocabulary of iconography and motifs, the same is by no means true of the poet or novelist. Anyone, even a woman, has to learn the language, and can commit personal experiences to paper in the privacy of one's room. Naturally this oversimplifies the

real difficulties and complexities involved in creating good or great literature... but it still gives a clue as to the possibility of the existence of an Emily Brontë or an Emily Dickinson, and the lack of their counterparts, at least until quite recently, in the visual arts. (Nochlin, 1988: 163)

Questioning the validity of the canon led feminist critics to research the work of previously neglected women artists (Gouma-Peterson and Matthews, 1987; Kreisel, 1999). Perhaps even more important than the discovery of previously unrecognized female artists was the re-evaluation of an entire area of visual art in which women excelled – that is, the crafts:

> A large part of traditional female creative output that conveyed a female experience had been invalidated as art and relegated to the category of 'craft' through the creation of an aesthetic hierarchy qualitatively differentiating 'high' from 'low' art. (Gouma-Peterson and Matthews, 1987: 332)

Critiques such as this led to considerable research on these female kinds of creative expression as valid and important kinds of art (ibid.: 333; see also Greer, 1979: 7; Hagaman, 1990).

As the changes in both literary and visual canons suggest, political and social considerations can weigh upon what is included and what is not. The point, in fact, can be made more generally. Although canons are in many ways peculiar to the arts, theoretical frameworks of all kinds involve implicit evaluations of what is worthy of research. If we look at medical research, for example, a field quite removed from research in the literary and visual arts, we can find some of the same kinds of evaluations. For many years the default gender for medical research was males. It was only 'in 1994 that the US National Institutes of Health (NIH) issued a guideline for the study and evaluation of gender differences in clinical trials' (Holdcroft, 2007: 2). Women had been excluded from the early studies of drugs even though the way that drugs affect women is sometimes quite different from the way they affect men (ibid.: 3). It should be noted that the use of men as the default subjects occurred not only in the United States but other countries as well (ibid.: 2–3).

The reason for the evaluations of what is worthy and what is not may or may not be related to social and political motivations and interests.

To some degree, the gender bias in medical research may have, for example, been based on monetary considerations: it was simply more costly to consider gender issues than to ignore them (ibid.). Nevertheless, whatever the motivations, we should not assume that what research focuses on is God-given. To the contrary, we should keep in mind that the selection of subjects worthy of consideration is based on assumptions and choices, conscious or unconscious, and that these assumptions may have significant implications for the conclusions that we can infer from the research.

Summary and concluding remarks

In this chapter we have examined the way in which theoretical paradigms – that is, the basic ideas and assumptions underlying research in a field – influence research activity. We have seen that at least the four following points about paradigmatic frameworks should be considered in critically assessing research.

- Research that is critical of work undertaken within a dominant theoretical paradigm may be subjected to more rigorous peer review than is the work it criticizes.

- A dominant theoretical paradigm may encourage research on certain questions and discourage research on other questions, even when investigations into these other questions could be fruitful.

- Research undertaken within a new paradigm may meet with resistance simply because it challenges a well-established paradigm.

- In fields such as literary and fine arts criticism, artistic canons function as dominant theoretical paradigms, serving to guide researchers about what is worth researching and what is not. In so doing, canons can discourage research on artistic activity that is not included in the canon.

None of this is to say that paradigms are some kind of pernicious impediment to independent research. Paradigms provide researchers in a field with coherent principles and a set of core research questions that scholars seek to investigate as thoroughly as possible. Still, to the extent that the ideological systems expressed by dominant paradigms shape the way researchers view their disciplines, there is the risk that they can result in tunnel vision on the part of researchers.

What do we mean by 'tunnel vision'? We use the phrase to describe the fact that a theoretical paradigm – an ideological system – can exert such a strong influence over scholars as to render a concept that is outside that paradigm almost unthinkable. We saw, for example, that Howard Gardner rejected the idea that intelligence is a unitary, heritable faculty. Nevertheless, the fact that he continued to accept the idea from the dominant paradigm that there is a sharp dichotomy between nature and nurture in the development of intelligence indicates the power of theoretical frameworks, even for someone who rejects some of the assumptions. The paradigm becomes the lens through which the researcher views phenomena. Moreover, the theoretical lens can crucially shape the view of not only an innovator but also research communities, sometimes affecting the way they handle innovations, as we saw in relation to the paradigm-changing research on ulcers of Marshall and his colleagues.

While that lens helps researchers to see phenomena and make theoretical sense of them, it can prevent them from seeing other phenomena that might be relevant. Nowhere is this perhaps more obvious than in relation to artistic canons, where paradigms of what can be considered important artistic artifacts can exclude large segments of significant artistic activity. Of course, as we noted, it is not only in the humanities that canon-like assumptions operate. What was the assumption that males are the default gender in medical research but a canon-like theoretical assumption?

Because they function as a lens through which phenomena are viewed, theoretical paradigms pose a challenge to non-experts who read about research and often make decisions based on its findings. Even if you have assured yourself that the research meets the gold standards, and taken into consideration the financial interests of both the scholars who conducted the research and those who funded it, it is prudent to consider that the way everyone sees something, even experts in a field, may not be the only way, and that what everybody 'knows' to be true may change because of ideas and facts outside our current range of vision.

Notes

1 Kuhn's classic work is entitled *The Structure of Scientific Revolutions*, and the examples he provides to substantiate his ideas are all taken from the realm of the physical sciences. Nevertheless, his account of how science progresses is widely applied to a diverse array of disciplines. To take but a few examples,

it has been applied to education (Bailey, 2006), sociology (Bryant, 1975), linguistics (Newmeyer, 1986) and literary criticism (Mailloux, 1978).

2   Ann Gibson (1993) makes an interesting observation concerning the participation of African Americans in art history programs. She notes that one of the departments where she had been an art history student had scholarship money reserved for a person of color. It went unused, however, because 'no person of color ever applied' (ibid.: 3). See, however, Bearden and Henderson (1993) for a comprehensive history of African American artists, which brings to light the unrecognized contributions of African Americans. See also Brawley (1937), as well as Meyerowitz (1997), who writes about a significant exhibition of African American artists.

5

The dissemination of research

Introduction

As we saw in the last chapter, a theoretical paradigm may predispose researchers to consider favorably those topics and conceptualizations that are compatible with it and to give less favorable treatment to those which are not. Paradigms, however, are not the only mechanism that can prevent research from being given full and just consideration. Just as important are the venues for disseminating research. Differing perspectives and new research topics are of very little significance if they have no venue through which to reach their audience.

In this chapter we look at three cases which bear directly on the issue of how research is disseminated. We first examine feminist research and research into homosexuality. We see how studies on gender and homosexuality that are based on non-traditional assumptions and perspectives have been published in new venues devoted specifically to this new research, presumably because established journals did not publish this kind of research. In the second case we once again look at pharmaceutical research, this time in relation to the suppression of unfavorable research findings. We examine how economic considerations can lead both companies and researchers to suppress research results which could have unfavorable economic consequences for them. Finally, we consider what is sometimes called 'gray literature' – that is, works in non-commercial publication venues. Although material published as gray literature may not be of interest to traditional publishers for economic or ideological reasons, it can nevertheless provide unique information and perspectives and thus constitute a significant resource when critically assessing research.

Case 1: research on homosexuality and feminist research

As we have seen, peer review is the process by which research manuscripts are scrutinized by the writer's professional peers in his or her specialty. It is, as we noted in the second chapter, one of the gold standards for academic and scientific research. A considerable level of objectivity is generally assumed to be conferred by the process: at least from a distance, the peer-review process is designed to ensure that the reports of research meet high standards of scholarship. Indeed, even a cursory examination of journals' and professional associations' claims about the process would lead one to believe that it is a neutral, objective way of determining whether or not research has value. Consider, for example, claims from the websites of two Elsevier publications from very different fields: the *Journal of English for Academic Purposes* and the *Annals of Physics*. The former proclaims that it

> practices a double blind peer review policy. The purpose of peer review is to ensure that only good research is published. Peer review is an objective process at the heart of good scholarly publishing and is carried out by all reputable academic journals. Our reviewers play a vital role in maintaining the high standards of the *Journal of English for Academic Purposes* and all manuscripts are peer reviewed... (*Journal of English for Academic Purposes*, 2009)

Similarly, the *Annals of Physics* website states:

> The practice of peer review is to ensure that good science is published. It is an objective process at the heart of good scholarly publishing and is carried out on all reputable scientific journals. Our referees therefore play a vital role in maintaining the high standards of *Annals of Physics* and all manuscripts are peer reviewed... (*Annals of Physics*, 2009)

This faith in peer review is hardly restricted to these two Elsevier publications. A study commissioned by the Publishing Research Consortium found that an overwhelming majority of the researchers it surveyed 'agreed that peer review greatly helps scientific communication and most (83%) believe that without peer review there would be no control' (Mark Ware Consulting, 2008: 1).

This same faith is also reflected in the way many libraries present the peer-review process. The library of the University at Buffalo (State University of New York), for example, states in one of its tutorials, 'If a scholarly article has been *peer reviewed*, that means it has gone through a process in which a panel board of experts (usually other academics) have reviewed its contents and decided it was suitable for publication' (University at Buffalo Libraries, undated).

One might assume given this widespread approval of the process that peer review would not only help to ensure that high-quality research is published in peer-reviewed journals, but also allow for various perspectives as long as the research is of high quality. An examination of two areas of scholarship that challenge prevailing theoretical paradigms, queer theory and feminist theory, suggest that this may not always be the case.

If a topic arouses strong negative reactions, those reactions may affect the kind of research undertaken about that topic. Homosexuality is one such topic. In many cultures, homosexuality and homosexuals have been the subject of revulsion, contempt, oppression and pity, attitudes from which scientists and scholars are not immune. Indeed, until 1973 homosexuality was classified by the American Psychiatric Association's *Diagnostic and Statistical Manual of Mental Disorders* as a psychiatric disorder. It was reclassified in the 1973 edition of this authoritative manual as 'Sexual orientation disturbance [Homosexuality]' (American Psychiatric Association, 1973: 44).

In Chapter 4 we saw that changes in the literary and fine arts canons were prompted by social and political movements, particularly the black liberation and feminist movements. Likewise, the compilers of the *Diagnostic and Statistical Manual of Mental Disorders* in the American Psychiatric Association did not wake up one day in 1973 and decide that they had been incorrect to view homosexuality as a mental disorder. Rather, the gay liberation movement was a significant impetus motivating the change (De Cecco, 1987: 106). The negative attitudes towards homosexuality were even then quite strong: despite its success in getting homosexuality reclassified, the gay liberation movement did not succeed in getting it removed completely from the *Manual* (ibid.: 107).

Taboos surrounding the very concept of homosexuality are long-standing, widespread and persistent. Various forms of legal discrimination against homosexuals exist in countries around the world (Stein, 1999: 284). In the United States, many states outlawed same-sex sexual activity (ibid.: 279–83) until 2003, when a ruling by the US

Supreme Court recognized the right of homosexuals to engage in consensual sexual activity (Bantley, 2008: 548).

These negative attitudes are reflected in both writing and research on this topic, as well as in the way work on this topic is received. Let's consider just a few examples. John Broderick's book *The Pilgrimage*, containing a frank treatment of homosexuality, was banned in Ireland in 1961 (Drisceoil, 2005: 156). A 1978 article on homosexuality in seventeenth-century New England notes that, although studies on sensitive topics such as adultery, divorce and pre-marital sex were beginning to appear, there was little information on variant sexual activity such as homosexuality, despite clear evidence that homosexuality existed in colonial New England (Oaks, 1978). Homosexuality was apparently not considered a topic for scholarly discourse.

A 1995 article in the journal *American Anthropologist* describes homosexuality as being so far beneath the radar screen of research undertaken within the academy that it has resulted in what the author describes as the 'homoabsentia' and 'homoamnesia' of anthropological and historical research (Roscoe, 1995). As a prime example, he describes the lack of recognition on the part of the eminent anthropologist Claude Lévi-Strauss of the androgyny of a significant dual-gendered deity in the mythology of the Zuni (Native Americans of the Southwestern United States). To illustrate Lévi-Strauss's negative views on homosexuality, the article notes his description of the largely gay resort of Fire Island, NY, as the 'oddest site to be found anywhere on the globe', to which people are drawn 'by its wholesale inversion of the normal conditions of life' (ibid.: 449). The article also points out that the historian Hayden White completely ignored the existence of homosexual activity in his discussion of the European view of the sexual practices of Indians in the New World. 'Nothing within the social and intellectual worlds of Lévi-Strauss or White,' the article states, 'gave them reason to think twice about passing over evidence concerning homosexuality' (ibid.: 450).

Nevertheless, despite such attitudes a gay liberation movement, comparable to the feminist movement and the African American struggle for rights and respect, began in the late 1960s. Although in the United States the Stonewall riots in New York City are often identified as the symbolic beginning of the movement, its actual beginning may be considered to predate that event (Prince, 2004: 62; Jagose, 1996: 30ff; Stein, 1999: 9). What was especially significant about this movement was that, unlike previous social movements that were essentially asking for acceptance of homosexuality, gay liberation was predicated upon a sense of pride, a sense that homosexuality was not something that should be simply tolerated but that it could be the basis of a positive sense of identity (Jagose, 1996: 32).

From this movement came perspectives on homosexuality that were quite different from the mainstream views briefly described above:

> Gay men, lesbians, and their allies began to openly and self-consciously study themselves and how they were represented in history and culture. This has led them to inquire how sex and sexual orientations have been and are constructed and conceptualized. The resulting field of lesbian and gay studies examines same-sex desires, preferences, orientations, erotics, lifestyles, sentiments and conceptions – how they differ (and remain the same) when the variables of time, place, culture, gender, class, race, and so forth are changed; how they are constructed and interpreted; and how they interact with other human phenomena such as law, scientific inquiry, medicine, government, art, popular culture, family and education... (Stein, 1999: 10)

Clearly, studies related to the social construction of gender, desire, lifestyles and attitudes would normally fall within the realm of the social sciences. However, given the attitudes of mainstream social science and psychology towards homosexuality, it is perhaps not surprising that much of the research emanating from lesbian and gay studies was not published in the mainstream journals but rather in new journals specifically devoted to these perspectives. In fact, these journals would seem to have arisen specifically to meet the demand for publishing venues for this new scholarship. A search in *Ulrichsweb*, a standard directory of periodicals, shows that of the 13 scholarly, peer-reviewed journals that result from a search under the subject search term 'homosexuality', not a single one has a start year before 1974 and the vast majority were created in the 1990s.

Was this upsurge in interest in this field reflected in a similar upsurge in interest in mainstream sociology journals? A cursory investigation of two mainstream publications, the *British Journal of Sociology* and the *American Journal of Sociology*, would suggest otherwise. A search of titles and abstracts in the *British Journal of Sociology* from 1999 to the present resulted in only one title with the search term 'homosex*' (the asterisk allowing for any letter combination following the stipulated letters) and only one title with the search term 'gay'. Similarly, an online search of the *American Journal of Sociology* from 1895 to 2003 resulted in only two full articles with titles containing the search term 'homosex*' and only one title with the search term 'gay'. Even given the limitations of such searches and the very real possibility that more in-depth searching of these and other journals might yield more articles, the searches suggest that mainstream sociology journals do not publish very much on these topics from any perspective. The point here is not that traditional mainstream social sciences publications have suppressed research undertaken from this new perspective, but rather that research on gays and lesbians is far from fully represented within the mainstream peer-reviewed journals, even though there has clearly been a significant amount of scholarly research in this area.

Why would the more traditional publications include relatively little research on homosexuality? A thorough attempt to answer this question is beyond the scope of this book, but a brief exploration of possible explanations will help to highlight issues about publication pertinent to our concerns.

While it is possible, it seems unlikely that there is little or no work that meets the standards of the traditional journals. More likely, the absence of published research on this topic in such journals stems from the negative attitudes towards homosexuality outlined above. It should be noted that this does not necessarily mean that there has been a policy on the part of any journal; it might simply be an inheritance from the traditional hostility. Researchers look for journals that publish articles in their areas of interest. If a journal does not, then researchers are likely to submit manuscripts to other journals that have shown interest. No conscious policy need be in play.

In addition, the theoretical paradigms of queer theory and critical studies in which most research on homosexuality is now situated may not be accepted by traditional social science journals. As we saw in the last chapter, adherence to one paradigm may lead to the rejection of others. While we are in no position to say whether this or other explanations are valid in this case, it does seem a likely reason for the growth of new journals to accommodate research on homosexuality.

Feminist scholarship confronts many of the same issues as scholarship on homosexuality. Although women never faced the overt hostility that homosexuals have, research and scholarship were for a long time the almost exclusive purview of males: it was males who produced the knowledge, the subject of which was similarly almost exclusively males. We saw that the expansion of venues for research on homosexuality was a product of the gay liberation movement. In the same way, the field of women's studies rose from virtual non-existence as of the early 1960s, and grew to the point where it was quite well established in colleges and universities by the 1990s, an increase that parallels the ascendancy of the feminist movement (Kessler-Harris, 2007).

In addition, feminist scholars have argued that women's contributions to history and intellectual thought have been devalued and overlooked by men: 'What was "known" about women was invariably formulated by men who quite clearly didn't know or didn't care about women's lives and women's realities' (Kramarae and Spender, 1992: 2).

Regardless of the accuracy of that claim, scholarship undertaken within the rubric of women's studies has faced obstacles that go beyond any explicit contempt, ignorance or indifference. In advocating the need for women's studies as a distinct area of research, feminist scholars have pointed to subtle but persistent institutional barriers that devalued the study of women, undertaken from a female point of view, as a legitimate object of inquiry within the humanities and social sciences:

> Western intellectual tradition which had for so long dominated the citadels of learning was relatively disinterested in the lives of women, apart that is from the anthropomorphic interest extended to the curious creature 'Woman' which demarcated the 'known' world from the realm of the natural, and measured the scope of (male) rationality. In the main... the Western tradition had neither sympathy for, nor curiosity about, the questions 'represented' by women... Broadly speaking the community of scholars had chosen not to critically engage with the predicaments of women not least because it was reliant on deploying the category of woman as a marker of the parameters of the domain of rational discourse. Necessarily then the feminist intellectual project had to 'restore the female half of humanity as a proper and necessary topic of social science, historical research and cultural analysis.'[1] (Crowley, 1999: 132)

A second, related institutional barrier to feminist scholarship is the structural organization of the academy. The organizing principle of institutions of higher education is the academic department. Each academic department is taken to be the unit within which a particular discipline is taught and studied. Feminist scholarship, on the other hand, does not have an obvious home within any academic department. It can perhaps best be understood as asking questions that draw on the disciplinary structures of such diverse fields as literature, psychology, sociology, anthropology, science, medicine, law and history. In other words, feminist scholarship inherently draws on 'cross-disciplinary and multi- or pluridisciplinary, as well as transdisciplinary, approaches; it also demands recognition... that the advancement of the collective bodies of knowledge available to us cannot proceed as if the existing disciplines comprised the ultimate, and only, modes of knowledge' (Boxer, 2000: 125).

Nevertheless, although women's studies research cuts across traditional disciplinary boundaries, it adds a unique contribution to disciplinary studies: research undertaken by women about women (Crowley, 1999). This research not only challenges traditional conceptions of *who* does research *about* whom, it also challenges traditionally accepted notions of what constitutes legitimate research questions. The premise and rationale underlying the claim for a unique contribution of women's studies are that simply expanding research in the disciplines to include women does little to alter traditional beliefs about what constitutes useful and valuable knowledge. Feminist scholarship advocates new research models that 'challenge the way knowledge is conceptualized and what is considered worth learning' (Tetreault, 1985: 367).

It is not surprising, then, that new scholarly journals developed in response to the demand for publication venues created by the burgeoning interest in scholarship in women's studies. In a discussion of the treatment of women's studies focused largely on the United States and France, Paula Schwartz (2002) notes a proliferation of journals that specialize in this area, beginning in the 1970s. A search in *Ulrichsweb* for peer-reviewed journals classified with the subject 'women's studies' returned 123 journals, only two of which began publication prior to the 1970s. Nineteen journals specializing in women's studies, from several countries, began publication in the 1970s, but the overwhelming majority began publishing in the 1980s and 1990s; 16 journals began publication between 2000 and 2009.

An assessment of research that relates to women cannot be restricted to an examination of research in traditional discipline journals. Regardless of the reasons, one thing is clear: not all work that is worthy and relevant to women is going to be published in the traditional peer-reviewed disciplinary journals. In the critical assessment of research, restricting oneself to the traditional publishing venues means potentially missing important critiques and perspectives.

In fact, for both women's and gay and lesbian studies, so much significant research has been published outside of the established traditional journals that to ignore these newer publication venues is to ignore work that has changed perspectives on research related to these groups in profound ways. One cannot understand Krafft-Ebing's (1965) famous research on homosexuality as a sexual perversion at this point in time without referring to gay and lesbian studies research on this topic found in contemporary gay and lesbian scholarly journals. Nor can one study research related to women's social roles without the context and theories introduced in contemporary women's studies journals that focus on this topic.

Case 2: pharmaceutical research

If ideology and values may be said to be the crux of the publication issues related to gay and feminist studies, the same cannot be said of publication issues related to pharmaceutical research. As we will see, in this case financial interests play a surprisingly significant role in what is published and what is not.

Consider the case of research related to antidepressants. A 2008 study published in the *New England Journal of Medicine* examined both the published and unpublished research on 12 antidepressant drugs. It found that 'The questions of whether the studies were published and, if so, how the results were reported were strongly related to their overall outcomes' (Turner et al., 2008: 254). Indeed, the relationship between publication and research outcomes was a straightforward one. Based on an examination of the evidence, the authors concluded that there was 'a bias toward the publication of positive results. Not only were positive results more likely to be published, but studies that were not positive, in... [the authors'] opinion, were often published in a way that conveyed a positive outcome' (ibid.: 256). The authors further suggest that this has led to published reports giving a considerably different impression than one would get from considering all of the research, both published and unpublished: 'we found that the efficacy of this drug class is less than would be gleaned from an examination of the published literature alone. According to the published literature, the results of nearly all of the trials of antidepressants were positive. In contrast, the Food and Drug Administration (FDA) analysis of the trial data showed that roughly half of the trials had positive results' (ibid.).

Why was so much significant research left unpublished? The authors of the study do not speculate. They do point out, however, that although one might claim that at least some of the research was not published because of 'methodological flaws', it should be noted 'the protocols were written according to international guidelines for efficacy studies and were carried out by companies with ample financial and human resources' (ibid.: 259).

While the authors of the study demur from speculating about the reasons for their findings, it is nevertheless clear that the research examined in the study had one common feature that could be seen as playing a major role: it was all sponsored by companies that had much to gain from research that supported the hypothesis that the antidepressants were effective. And since the researchers benefited from the support of the pharmaceutical companies, they too had a financial stake in the outcomes for the simple reason that their benefactors did.

Concerns about conflicts of interest, in fact, led the *New England Journal of Medicine* to declare in the early 1990s that authors writing reviews and editorials on published research – that is, those with the responsibility of shaping evaluative opinion of the work – could not have any financial ties that might result in a conflict of interest. Thus the 'Information for authors' stated:

> Because the essence of reviews and editorials is selection and interpretation of the literature, the *Journal* expects that authors of such articles will not have any financial interest in a company (or its competitor) that makes a product discussed in the article. (Drazen and Curfman, 2002: 1901)

Nevertheless, a decade later the *New England Journal of Medicine* had to revisit its prohibition because it was unable to find enough authors without any financial interests. The new policy stated that the authors should not have any 'significant interest in a company (or a competitor) that makes a product discussed in the article' (ibid.).

The effect that the earlier prohibition had on the potential pool of authors is not surprising since there has been a growing dependency of research on the pharmaceutical industry for its very life-blood. Beginning in the 1980s, there has been pressure on universities and hospitals to seek research funding from private industry (Baird, 2003). In fact, the pharmaceutical industry has become the largest sponsor of medical research in Great Britain, Canada and the United States (Collier and Iheanacho, 2002: 1407).

Although the cooperation between academic research and industry can lead to fruitful discoveries of safe and effective medications, it inevitably leads to conflicts of interest (Baird, 2003). As noted in a report by the US Congress Office of Technology Assessment (1998: 114), 'it is possible that university-industry relationships could adversely affect the academic environment of universities by inhibiting the free exchange of scientific information... or delaying or completely impeding publication of research results'. That the possibility referred to in this report is more than theoretical is borne out by a survey of life sciences faculty from the 50 universities that received the most funding from the National Institutes of Health in 1993. The survey was designed to measure whether or not these scientists withheld significant research findings. According to the survey:

> One-fifth reported that they had delayed publication for more than 6 months during the past 3 years to allow for patent application or negotiation, to resolve intellectual property rights disputes, to protect their scientific lead over competitors, or to slow the distribution of undesired results. Almost one in ten had refused to share research results with other scientists during the past 3 years. Delays in publication were associated with participation in a research relationship with industry and with commercialization of one's own research results. (Warner and Gluck, 2003: 41)

The point here is that not only the pharmaceutical industry but also many researchers have financial interests in the research they undertake. Given a growing relationship between researchers and industry, it is not surprising that there was less enthusiasm in general for antidepressant research with outcomes that were not favorable to the product being investigated.

Smoking guns in these matters are not always easy to find, and in the case of the antidepressant research there may not have been any conscious conspiracy to suppress publication. Still, in some cases there is clear evidence that companies, sometimes aided and abetted by researchers, did attempt to suppress the publication of drug-study outcomes that were not what they wished.

The story behind COX-2 (cyclooxygenase-2) drugs such as Celebrex and Vioxx serves as a good example of deliberate suppression. Unlike the case of antidepressants, the evidence is reasonably clear that pharmaceutical company researchers in this case cherry-picked data, ignoring findings that suggested problems and selecting for publication results that gave a misleading impression.

COX-2 drugs such as Celebrex and Vioxx belong to the broad class of NSAIDs (non-steroidal anti-inflammatory drugs), including ibuprofen and naproxen, which are commonly used to treat arthritis (Brody, 2007;

Dohrman, 2005). However, while these older NSAIDs effectively reduced the pain and inflammation of conditions like arthritis, they had the serious side-effect of increasing the risk of ulcers (Brody, 2007; Dohrman, 2005; Wright, 2002). The COX-2 drugs, which were developed in the 1990s, were marketed as an improvement over the older NSAIDs because they reduced the pain and inflammation of arthritis with a reduced risk of ulcers (Brody, 2007).

The Celecoxib Long-term Arthritis Safety Study (CLASS), which was published in *JAMA* in September 2000, compared Celebrex with the traditional NSAIDs for incidence of ulcers and other adverse side-effects. The article was written by 16 authors, of whom six were employed by Pharmacia, the manufacture of Celebrex,[2] and the rest were paid consultants to Pharmacia (ibid.: 107). CLASS was a rigorous scientific study, involving over 8,000 subjects in the United States and Canada between September 1998 and March 2000, and the *JAMA* article gave every appearance of being an unbiased report of its findings. The study compared patients receiving the two alternative drugs 'during the 6-month treatment period' (Silverstein et al., 2000: 1247). The findings of the CLASS study as reported in *JAMA* were highly positive for Celebrex. The study concluded that subjects who were treated with Celebrex – at relatively high dosages – experienced significantly fewer ulcers than those taking the older NSAIDs. It also found that the group treated with Celebrex did not experience a greater degree of 'cardiovascular events' – heart attack and stroke – than those using the older NSAIDs (ibid.).

Michael Wolfe, one of the editors of *JAMA*, was favorably impressed with the drug when the CLASS article was submitted to the journal. He was the co-author of a cautiously positive editorial about the article (Lichtenstein and Wolfe, 2000). However, in 2001, as a member of the FDA's advisory committee on arthritis, Wolfe had occasion to examine the entire data set from the CLASS study on the FDA website (Brody, 2007: 108; Okie, 2001).[3] He learned that the whole CLASS study lasted over a year, rather than the six months reported in the article, and that a review of the complete data set led to different conclusions about the safety and efficacy of Celebrex than those arrived at by the authors of the CLASS article. A *Washington Post* article discussing the missing data quotes Wolfe as saying, 'I am furious... I wrote the editorial. I looked like a fool. But... all I had available to me was the data presented in the article' (Okie, 2001).

To be sure, Pharmacia denied that there was any attempt to mislead in the selection of the data. Stephen Geis, one of the authors of the *JAMA* article and the vice-president for clinical research of Pharmacia, claimed that after six months 'more patients withdrew from the comparison groups than from the Celebrex group, biasing later findings'. According to Geis, 'the intention really was not to be deceptive in any way… People thought that six months was the appropriate analysis' (ibid.). Still, the unreported data were significant. Based on the data set, the FDA concluded that Celebrex had no safety advantages over the older NSAIDs (ibid.).

The FDA was not alone in drawing less favorable conclusions from the complete data set. Looking at the entire set of data from the CLASS study, as well as data from another study (Bombardier et al., 2000), another researcher, James Wright, compared the COX-2 drugs with the older NSAIDs with respect to death rates. He found that the 'incidence of serious adverse events, including death, admission to hospital, and any life threatening event or event leading to serious disability, was significantly higher with COX-2 selective NSAIDs than with nonselective NSAIDs' (Wright, 2002: 1133). He noted specifically an increased risk of 'thrombotic cardiovascular' events that 'more than cancels out the reduction in absolute risk of complicated ulcers' (ibid.: 1135).

Wright (ibid.: 1131) also noted that the data that had been left out of the original *JAMA* article reporting on the research led to a different set of conclusions than those reached by the authors. Despite the claim that there was a valid reason for examining only the smaller data set, the simple fact remains that the authors did not even mention the larger set and in effect they were actively suppressing the dissemination of research results by not explicitly addressing the issue of data sets.

Let us now turn to an example where an article written for publication was suppressed not by researchers but by the pharmaceutical company itself. Betty Dong, a researcher at the University of California Medical Center, San Francisco, compared the efficacy of three forms of the generic drug levothyroxine in treating hypothyroidism with the brand-name drug Synthroid, which was manufactured by Boots Pharmaceuticals, the company that sponsored Dong's research (Brody, 2007). She found that, despite what physicians had commonly believed for many years, the three varieties of levothyroxine she studied were as effective as the more expensive Synthroid (McCarthy, 1997; Brody, 2007: 104). When Dong notified Boots of the results of her study in 1990, the company immediately set about discrediting her research (McCarthy, 1997), alleging that the study was fraught with errors and ethical lapses (Brody, 2007: 104).

Dong and her colleagues reported her findings in a paper submitted to *JAMA* in 1994 (McCarthy, 1997). The submission was accompanied by a letter from Dong to *JAMA*, in which she described her dispute with Boots and requested the editors not to select thyroid experts she knew of who were paid consultants of Boots to be peer reviewers for her paper. It turned out that, in the same way that the *New England Journal of Medicine* was forced to relax its prohibition on authors having financial relationships with the manufacturers of the drugs they review, *JAMA* had 'considerable trouble identifying suitable experts in thyroid disease who were competent to review the paper and were *not* paid consultants of Boots' (Brody, 2007: 104). Still, *JAMA* accepted the paper for publication after minor revisions. However, less than two weeks before the paper was scheduled to appear, Dong wrote to *JAMA* asking that the paper not be published, citing a contract she had signed with the company back in 1987 that required her to secure its written permission prior to publishing any results from the study (Vogel, 1997; Brody, 2007: 105). She cited 'impending legal action' by Boots (McCarthy, 1997).

In the meantime, an alternative analysis of Dong's data was published in the *American Journal of Therapeutics* by a scientist at Boots – and also, incidentally, an associate editor of that journal (Vogel, 1997; Brody, 2007: 105). The article did not mention Dong by name, nor did it acknowledge her analysis. The publication of this paper could have had the effect of forestalling the possibility of Dong's research ever being published, since medical journals prohibit the publication of duplicate data (Brody, ibid.). This would have meant that, although Dong's data were indeed published, her analysis would have been completely suppressed.

A front-page article exposing the dispute that appeared in the *Wall Street Journal* (King, 1996) was the impetus for a change in the ultimate fate of Dong's article. The *Wall Street Journal* article attracted the interest of the FDA, prompting it to exert pressure on the company to submit Dong's data to the agency (Brody, 2007: 105). The ultimate result of this pressure was that in 1997 Dong was permitted to publish in *JAMA* the identical paper that had been scheduled to appear two years earlier (ibid.: 106). That same issue of *JAMA* also included two letters to the editor by the company: one gave the company's version of what had transpired, and the other gave its arguments that Dong's research was flawed and her conclusions inaccurate (ibid.).

What conclusions can we take away from all of this? Even when research is performed by highly qualified researchers and published in respectable peer-reviewed medical journals, we cannot assume that the data or results presented are necessarily the whole story – especially when the findings may impact on the bottom line of the individuals and/or institutions that are parties to the research.

We are not suggesting that research performed by interested parties is useless or necessarily of poor quality. It is quite possible for individuals and institutions with an interest in the outcome of research to act in a disinterested way. Indeed, it is worth noting that in the case of the COX-2 drugs the actual research did have unadulterated outcomes. That said, when we examine articles reporting on research we do need to be aware that the complete context may be lacking and we must be careful not to assume that one article or even a set of articles is the final word. Responsible assessment of research must often proceed slowly, giving time for the consideration of results that may not yet have been disseminated but may nevertheless turn out to be of significant consequence.

Case 3: gray literature

Throughout this book we have been examining ways to contextualize research. We have argued that in assessing the value of research we cannot simply rely on the fact that the researchers are experts in their fields and the results are published in respectable venues in which the research is reviewed by peers. We have argued throughout that research must be understood and evaluated in context.

In this chapter we have been looking at the context of publication venues. In the first part of this chapter we saw how research is best viewed not only in relation to other research in similar journals but, at least at times, also in relation to research published in venues offering different perspectives and values. In the second part of this chapter we saw how peer-reviewed research should be seen not only in relation to other published work but also in relation to work that has possibly not been published at all, sometimes for reasons that have little or nothing to do with the quality of the research.

Although the two cases discussed above touch on different issues, they both relate to publication in peer-reviewed journals. However, not all important research that is published appears in peer-reviewed publications. There is, in fact, a substantial body of research in many different fields that does not appear at all in such venues. In this section we look at some of this research, specifically research that is disseminated in what is called 'gray literature'.

The standard definition of gray literature is 'Information produced on all levels of government, academics, business and industry in electronic and print formats not controlled by commercial publishing i.e. where publishing is not the primary activity of the producing body' (as quoted in GreyNet, 2009). In other words, gray literature is information that is distributed outside the normal commercial publication channels, including commercially produced peer-reviewed journals and scholarly books.

In order to get a better sense of what gray literature is, it is useful to consider one of its major institutional sources: foundations. Foundations play important roles around the world. Although they differ from country to country, we can for our purposes consider them all to have the following characteristics: they are all non-membership-based, non-profit organizations that are self-governing and whose mission is to serve some public purpose (Anheier, 2001: 3–4). The range of institutions that can be considered foundations under this definition is wide. It includes the German Robert Bosch Foundation (Robert Bosch Stiftung, undated.b) whose 'main purpose [is] public health care' but which also focuses on 'international understanding, welfare, education, the arts and culture, and research and teaching in the humanities, social sciences and natural sciences' (Robert Bosch Stiftung, undated.a). It also includes the Ford Foundation, which states that its mission is to 'Strengthen democratic values, Reduce poverty and injustice, Promote international cooperation, [and] Advance human achievement' (Ford Foundation, 2009).

While not all foundations participate in research activities, a significant number do. Foundations which do engage in research either have their own researchers or fund independent projects. Foundations which primarily have in-house scholars are often called think-tanks. The conservative American Enterprise Institute is such a foundation and claims on its website to be 'home to some of America's most accomplished public policy experts – from economics, law, political science, defense and foreign policy studies, ethics, theology, medicine, and other fields' (American Enterprise Institute, 2005). The Brookings Institution, a liberal American think-tank, also does its research through 'more than 200 resident and nonresident fellows' (Brookings Institution, undated). The Ford Foundation, on the other hand, focuses on external grants in many areas, including projects whose primary activity is research.

In either case, the research may be published in one of two ways. It may be published through the standard publication venues – for example, the journals published by the American Heart Association

(2009). Alternatively, it may be published independently of these standard venues, with the foundation itself functioning in the role of publisher and distributor of materials for which there is no charge. This latter means of dissemination of research is one of the major kinds of gray literature, an immensely important complement to the standard publication venues of peer-reviewed journals and scholarly books.

Not surprisingly, a substantial amount of the gray literature that originates from foundations advocates positions or values that are part of the foundation's mission. This is particularly true of foundations which have clear ideological missions, such as the Brookings Institution and the American Enterprise Institute. Much of the research in reports they disseminate is in articles and longer monographs that are clearly intended to support the ideological positions they advocate: an American conservative ideology in the case of the American Enterprise Institute and an American liberal ideology in the case of Brookings.

However, regardless of whether or not it is influenced by the specific mission of the sponsoring foundation, gray literature from foundations encompasses a wide range of topics. For example, the research reported in 'Liberal education and civic engagement' (Lawry et al., 2006), a report from a Ford Foundation-sponsored project, addresses the question of cultivating 'civic engagement' in American college and university students, while psychological health in the workplace is the concern of the *Early Intervention Following Trauma* report (Rick et al., 2006) published by the Institute for Employment Studies at the University of Sussex but copyrighted and distributed for free on the website of its foundation sponsor, the British Occupational Health Research Foundation.

Although foundations are a significant source of gray literature, they are by no means the only source. Gray literature includes everything from internal government and business reports to scientific and scholarly documents produced by both academics and researchers in corporate settings that are not intended for standard publication.

While much of this literature follows the forms and conventions of the standard publication venues, this is not necessarily the case. Consider the following by way of illustration. Microsoft engages in research and development, especially under the auspices of the company known as Microsoft Research, which employs 'more than 700 people at five labs on three continents' according to its website (Rashid, 2009). Although its researchers frequently publish in established journals, Microsoft Research also produces its own reports. One example is the 98-page report on its website entitled *Being Human: Human-Computer Interaction in the Year 2020* (Harper et al., 2008).

The report is based on the proceedings of a two-day conference in 2007 in Seville, Spain, that was sponsored by Microsoft Research. However, it is not a record of the papers presented or discussions held, but a distillation, an attempt to capture the spirit of what concerned and excited the participants, looking ahead to 2020. The report describes how the world around us has changed and continues to change, and how the design of computers is helping to create a new socio-digital landscape. It explains how the field of human-computer interaction can contribute to making this landscape one that reflects the values we hold as well as providing opportunities for the expression of diversity in those values (ibid.: 9).

This is not the stuff of which scholarly books are generally made. The report is speculative, and undertakes the kind of educated hypothesizing that one might find specialists informally engaging in. It does not attempt to support its contentions with careful documentation or formal argument. In fact, its bibliography is for some sections no more than a set of suggested readings.

Nevertheless, what the report does do is to explore the ways in which specialists in software development imagine the course of future development. It suggests that point-and-click mouse applications, for example, will be replaced with interactive designs that permit far more user functions (ibid.: 16ff). By providing us with ideas about where researchers in the field believe human-computer interaction development is likely to lead, it allows us to contextualize other research on this issue that addresses more specific concerns.

Academics also use gray literature venues at times rather than standard publication venues. Many post drafts of articles that they have not yet prepared for formal publication or which, for one reason or another, they are not interested in disseminating in a more formal manner.

Jan Koster (2009), for example, is a distinguished Dutch linguist who puts on his website not only digital versions of published articles but also articles which have never been published. Although identified as drafts, some of these articles are seven or more years old and would not appear to be moving from the draft to a published version any time soon (see, for example, Koster, 2000). Does this make the articles necessarily less useful or less authoritative than published material? We should not assume that this is the case. The reasons for research not being published, as we have seen, are many and disparate. While it is quite conceivable that the research is not in a form that meets the intellectual standards for publication, it is also possible that the editors of journals or books in the relevant discipline may not be interested in a particular topic or might not share the values or assumptions underlying the research.

Certainly, if a researcher has a proven track record over many years, the gray literature produced by that researcher may well be worthy of serious consideration. Indeed, the availability of a considerable number of 'unpublished' articles through such governmental venues as the American Education Resources Information Center (ERIC) (www.eric.ed.gov/), Science.gov (www.science.gov/index.html) and the National Research Council Canada (http://nparc.cisti-icist.nrc-cnrc.gc.ca/npsi/ctrl?lang=en) would suggest that work not published in traditional venues can be of significant interest.

Governments are not only gateways to gray literature but also a major source of such literature. Throughout the world governments issue reports on a wide variety of topics. Some of these simply present numerical data – as can be seen, for example, in many of the smaller reports on the US Bureau of Labor Statistics website (www.bls.gov) – while others are article- and book-length monographs, such as the British *Gowers Review of Intellectual Property* (Gowers, 2006).

On occasion these reports are published in traditional publishing venues and not as gray literature. One example is the British government's Stern Review report on *The Economics of Climate Change* (Stern, 2007). This 575-page report from the UK Treasury has been widely discussed in the media. Most reports, however, do not generate as much interest and are only distributed by the governments themselves as gray literature. Before the internet this generally meant print publication through a government printing office. The internet, particularly the web, however, has greatly increased accessibility, with many reports being offered in a downloadable form and, just as importantly, easily discovered through web searches.

Even this cursory examination of gray literature makes clear that this is not a publication venue that can be ignored. In fact, it is possible to state that in at least certain areas it is an absolute necessity to examine this kind of literature. Could economic research or its assessment do without government reports on economic activity? The importance of gray literature in this area predates the web by over a century. Consider the fact that Karl Marx's seminal economic work *Capital* (1990) relies heavily on the British Parliamentary Papers, which were gray literature reports of the time.

Even in the area of medicine, where publication in a peer-reviewed journal is almost always considered obligatory for research to be taken seriously, gray literature can play an important role. A study of the role of gray literature in research on schizophrenia concluded that while 'the use of grey literature does not always lead to less publication bias', nevertheless a 'comprehensive search for systematic reviews in schizophrenia should pay attention primarily to the former [that is, negative results] since these data have less chance of being published as formal literature' (Martin et al., 2005: 552; see also McAuley et al., 2000).

Gray literature offers a means of disseminating research of potentially high quality that may fall through the cracks in the standard network of scholarly publication. It can disseminate both scholarly articles and speculative thought-provoking literature that may be hard to publish in traditional venues. Gray literature is a means by which government agencies and the research laboratories in private corporations can circulate any research they deem appropriate to their mission and needs – without the need to sell their publications, the way a journal has to sell subscriptions or a publishing company has to sell books. It is the means through which individual scholars can distribute articles that may not be of direct interest to mainstream publications, even though they contribute to the knowledge base of a discipline. Gray literature thus promotes the dissemination of research free from the constraints of traditional publishing. When we need to view research through a critical lens, such alternative perspectives are invaluable.

Summary and concluding remarks

In this chapter we made the following points.

- Research involving new subjects of study or new theoretical paradigms may appear in new journals rather than established ones.
- Research findings may be suppressed by either researchers or funding organizations when the findings might have an adverse effect on their economic interests.
- Gray literature can help to fill gaps in the research record left by traditional publication venues.

These points are not meant to suggest that good research does not get disseminated in traditional venues. However, they do mean that not all good research gets disseminated in this way. Standard publications sometimes do not create environments in which challenges to a theoretical orthodoxy have the same publication opportunities as research supporting the prevailing view. Moreover, at times solid research findings are suppressed or only appear as gray literature. To be unaware of these potential gaps is to leave oneself open to the erroneous assumption that the conclusions reached by researchers published in traditional mainstream venues necessarily represent the full range of scholarly opinions, when, in fact, further investigation in other venues might lead to rather different conclusions.

In this chapter we have looked at a range of factors, extraneous to the quality of research itself, that can affect whether or not it is disseminated in traditional venues. The cases we have considered are indicative of how the dissemination of research and research results can be influenced by both dominant ideologies and financial interests.

We first looked at research based on new theoretical perspectives and ideologies that may not be found in the established journals in a field. Specifically, we discussed how research on homosexuality and women based on new perspectives grew in relation to social movements, and that this research found outlets not in traditional publications but rather in new journals developed to disseminate it. The gay liberation movement, with its rejection of the widely accepted view that homosexuality is a disorder, coupled with its advocacy of equality for homosexuality in every realm of society, provided a fertile soil for research on homosexuality undertaken from new vantage points. We saw that as this new research proliferated, there was a concomitant growth in the number of peer-reviewed journals devoted to gay studies which provided venues for disseminating it. Similarly, a new kind of research on women developed in response to a growing feminist movement. This research challenged prevailing conceptions both about gender and about the intellectual contributions of women. Here, too, new journals were developed to accommodate the research. We suggested that to assess research pertaining to these groups, it is necessary to take into consideration not only work published in traditional journals but research in these newer journals as well.

We also noted that what is published in the standard venues can be influenced by financial considerations. We looked at one example in which a pharmaceutical company – Boots – asserted its right to control the dissemination of research it sponsored by requiring the researcher, Betty Dong, to agree to the company's right to review any work emanating from that research prior to publication. Boots invoked its right of prior review to suppress the publication of Dong's research results because her findings threatened the predominant position of its product, Synthroid, and were therefore detrimental to the financial interests of the company. Although publicity about the dispute ultimately led to the publication of Dong's research, such publicity is not standard. It is important to bear in mind, therefore, that what appears in mainstream publication venues may not in some cases be a comprehensive representation of research findings.

The story of research on the COX-2 drugs is suggestive of a somewhat more complex situation. Here it was the researchers – all of whom were either employed by or paid consultants to the manufacturer, Pharmacia – who suppressed aspects of their own research data which were not favorable to the product they investigated. Again, this illustrates the need to be mindful that peer-review journal articles do not always tell the complete story.

Like new journals, gray literature, we suggested, is a significant source of additional information and perspectives. How important are these perspectives? Consider that at least one review of the literature suggested that less favorable studies of medications for schizophrenia tended to be published not in commercial peer-reviewed journals but only as gray literature. These less favorable results could raise doubts about the efficacy of these medications that would not likely arise by simply considering the research published in the peer-reviewed journals. Moreover, in many fields the data found in gray literature venues provide crucial information for both research and its assessment. Consideration of such venues should not be ignored simply because they do not meet all of the gold standards for evaluating research.

Notes

1 The quotation Crowley uses is originally from de Groot and Maynard (1993).
2 Pharmacia was purchased by Pfizer in April 2003 (Dow Jones News Service, 2003).
3 The researchers were legally required to submit the complete data set to the FDA (Brody, 2007: 108).

6

Moving beyond the gold standards: tools and techniques

Introduction

In the last three chapters we looked at some of the ways that research can be influenced by economic and ideological interests – factors that are supposedly extraneous to the work of science and scholarship. Our aim in examining these cases was to call attention to some of the potentially problematic issues that can affect research. Awareness of these issues does not by itself, however, provide us with the information we need for critical assessment. It is one thing to be aware that financial conflicts of interest may affect either the research itself or its dissemination; it is another to search for and find information that may help us to see if in a particular case there is indeed such a conflict of interest. We may suspect that there are paradigms other than the one used in some research report; to find out about other paradigms is far more challenging.

For someone who is not an expert in a field of research – and as we pointed out at the beginning of this book, that is almost all of us almost all of the time – critically assessing research can seem a daunting task. Clearly, viewing research in a more complete context so that we can see not only its strengths but also its limitations can very well be a time-consuming task, and not one that we are going to want to undertake every time there is a new research finding reported in the media. To the contrary, we would expect that undertaking a critical assessment of research is more likely to be the exception in our lives than the norm.

Still, there are going to be times when we need to look at research findings with a critical eye. School assignments are, of course, an occasion when you may need to assess research critically, but it is far from the only occasion. It may be a personal need: a time, for example, when you or someone you know is sick and you need to find out about the newest drugs to treat a disease, or a time when you need to make sure you are making sound investments. It may be a work-related need: a time when you must look carefully at the research about a community or a particular group of people. On all of these occasions you need to know not only that there may potentially be reasons for skepticism about research and how it is reported, but also how to locate the information you need to assess it critically.

Much of this chapter is devoted to exploring techniques and strategies that can be used to help uncover the information you need. We will first talk about how you can find out whether the research you are looking at meets the gold standards. However, in order to contextualize research, we need to go beyond the gold standards. We also need to look at research in terms of ideological interests (including the theoretical paradigms researchers adhere to) and financial interests, both of which may affect the research itself as well as our understanding of it. For this reason, in addition to looking at ways of finding information about whether or not research meets the gold standards, our focus in this chapter includes the methods and techniques for locating the information required to identify the economic and ideological contexts within which the research is undertaken.

Let us first discuss how to find information to determine whether research meets the gold standards. In Chapter 2 we identified three gold standards for assessing research: peer review, the reputation of the publisher and the credentials of the author. Let us look at each standard in turn.

Determining the credentials of the author is usually a straightforward process. Scholarly articles invariably contain some information about the author in the article: the college, university, laboratory or think-tank with which he or she is affiliated, as well as his or her position within the organization (for example, a department in the case of a college or university or area of specialization in the case of a think-tank or laboratory). Information about the author is also provided in books: it is often given on the book jacket, although it is sometimes found in introductory material inside the book itself.

Libraries sometimes remove the book jacket even though it contains information about the author. In this case you can consult directories such as *Who's Who* or the *National Faculty Directory*, both of which are usually available in the reference sections of academic libraries. Alternatively, a simple web search using an internet search engine will often reveal the author's professional affiliation and position.

The reputation of the publisher may be trickier to determine. University presses are almost always considered reputable publishers, as are the journals of highly regarded professional associations, such as *JAMA*, which is published by the American Medical Association. In the less obvious cases, however, it sometimes requires a bit of knowledge about a field or about academia to know which are the most prestigious publishing companies. In the case of books, determining the reputation of a publisher may be a matter of observation: noticing that an academic library or university bookstore tends to have books by certain publishers is usually a good indication that those are reputable companies. In addition, a web search can be useful here. Locating a publisher's website and seeing what kinds of books are listed there will give you some indication of the scholarly reputation of the publisher.

Let us now turn to peer review. The peer review of a journal article or a scholarly or scientific book, as we noted in Chapter 2, is generally considered to be the hallmark of the gold standards. How can we tell if an article or book meets that gold standard? In an academic environment, one highly regarded means of identifying peer-reviewed journals is to use a directory of periodicals called *Ulrich's*, which also exists as an online product called *Ulrichsweb*. You simply look up the journal by title in *Ulrich's* – using either format – and it will state whether or not the journal is peer reviewed.

While this is a standard method, it is by no means the only one available. In fact, most of the time all that is necessary to find out whether or not a journal is peer reviewed is a computer and an internet connection. You can use any of the well-known search engines to find the homepage of the journal. In almost all cases, a journal which is peer reviewed will state as much either on its homepage or on a page of instructions for authors.

There are, in fact, times when this simple do-it-yourself method is actually more informative than using a standard reference such as *Ulrich's*. Examining the homepage of a journal can sometimes reveal significant details about the journal editors' interpretation of peer review. Sometimes you may find out, for example, that the journal only publishes articles by authors who are members of the professional association that publishes the journal. Alternatively a journal may restrict publication to articles based on papers that were delivered at a particular conference. With this type of publication policy, the reviewers have a smaller set of manuscripts from which to select than they would if the potential pool of authors were not restricted.

Moreover, even if the journal adheres to the most rigorous interpretation of peer review, not all articles in that journal are necessarily peer reviewed. Peer-reviewed journals sometimes publish articles – commentaries and editorials, for example – that are not subjected to the peer-review process, unlike the other articles in the journal.

It is important to bear in mind, then, that simply knowing that a journal is peer reviewed is not always sufficient: peer review is subject to different interpretations and, additionally, it cannot be assumed that every article in a peer-reviewed journal has necessarily been peer reviewed. Examining the actual selection policy of a journal, as well as the characteristics of specific articles, can sometimes provide a far better idea of how the journal actually goes about selecting texts than the label 'peer reviewed' could possibly convey.

Identifying scholarly books is far more problematic. Rarely will a book publisher talk about the selection process for research monographs in the explicit manner that is at this point common practice for journals. What complicates the issue even more is that the same publisher or imprint that publishes serious research reports may publish far less serious work as well. This is even true of university presses, which now at times publish trade publications such as popular histories as well as the extended monographs characteristic of serious research.

What information, then, can help you identify which books are scholarly, analogous to the information available to distinguish peer-reviewed from non-peer-reviewed journals? Asking these three sets of questions can help.

- What are the credentials of the author? Does the author have a proven track record in the areas in which he or she is writing? Is the writer actually an expert in the field rather than in another field, without any claim to expertise in the topic at hand?

- Are the claims about the research backed up by explicit documentation through citing the work of others and/or providing original research data?

- Does the introduction or preface suggest that it is written for experts or is it rather a 'dumbed-down' volume intended only for general readers that clearly does not provide the kind of evidence or arguments specialists in the field could accept?

In fact, as we have seen, given the variety of ways in which the term 'peer reviewed' is applied to journals, these are probably good questions to ask about the articles in peer-reviewed journals as well.

Financial research on publicly traded companies is perhaps even less transparent and more susceptible to uneven quality control. Accounting standards are supposed to prevent inappropriate research reports on companies' financial health, and in many countries, including the United States and United Kingdom, there are professional bodies whose role is to enforce these standards (Fearnley et al., 2005).

Nevertheless, as we saw in Chapter 3 in our discussion of Enron, the accounting firms that evaluate the financial reports of companies have a complex financial relationship with these companies: these companies are both the subject of the research performed by the accounting firms and a significant source of their income. The nature of this relationship can often corrupt what is supposed to be a disinterested assessment of a company's finances.

The Enron case and the more recent sub-prime crisis serve as stark reminders of the limitations of the gold standards: even if research apparently meets the standards of professional review, even if it is explicitly documented and the credentials of the researchers are impeccable, issues related to money and values can distort the research process. Moreover, as we have shown elsewhere in this book, the limitations of the gold standards are not unique to any one field of endeavor. In Chapters 3–5 we saw examples from various disciplines, ranging from the pharmaceutical field to the social sciences and the humanities, of research being influenced by economic and ideological interests, even though it met all of the gold-standard criteria.

As we have seen, then, to assess research critically, especially in areas in which we are not experts, we need to go beyond the gold standards and look more carefully at the context of the research. We need to be particularly aware of the possible role that money and values may have played in influencing the research. But how does one go about this without spending inordinate amounts of time in the process?

Investigating research

Whether you are looking to investigate the possibility of financial conflicts of interest or you suspect that there may be alternative ideological perspectives from which to view a topic, there are basic methods you can use to uncover what may not be apparent in the research. There are three main resources for investigation:

- newspapers and magazines
- Web 2.0: blogs, wikis, social networking sites and the references and resources which are often mentioned in them
- scholarly material: scholarly books and journals (including open access journals), gray literature and the reference lists contained in all of these resources.

We will look at each of these in turn.

Newspapers and magazines

Conflicts of interest involving financial motivations can be uncovered, for the most part, in one of two ways. You may uncover potential conflicts directly by looking for evidence of financial incentives that may have affected the research, or you may try to find evidence that has been ignored or glossed over by the research you are considering.

In both cases, newspapers and popular magazines can be useful sources of information. As we saw in the third chapter, newspapers uncovered valuable information about the funding of the work of Robert Wilson, the most influential advocate of hormone replacement therapy: a *Boston Globe* article reported that Wilson's son, Ronald, stated that his father's work had been supported by the drug company that manufactured the primary hormone used in the therapy.

Attempts to suppress research data or to 'spin' the findings are also sometimes revealed through the mass media. It was, for example, an article in the *Wall Street Journal* that alerted the FDA to the fact that a pharmaceutical company had suppressed the publication of Betty Dong's research showing that generic varieties were as effective as the brand-name drug Synthroid in treating hypothyroid disease.

Newspapers and magazines can also help to reveal corrupt reporting practices in the financial area. It is worth noting that one of the first hints of trouble about Enron came from a *Fortune* magazine article by Bethany McLean (2001) entitled 'Is Enron overpriced?'. Considering that at the time Enron was thought by most experts to be a nearly perfect company, this article took a great deal of perspicuity and courage to write – especially when you keep in mind that the financial reports of Arthur Andersen's accountants did their best to hide the true state of affairs.

Ideological influence can also be uncovered by newspapers looking at sources of financial support for researchers. Charles Murray and Richard Herrnstein acknowledge the support of the American Enterprise Institute in the acknowledgements in *The Bell Curve*. What is not acknowledged is the source of funding that enabled the American Enterprise Institute to retain Charles Murray as a research fellow. This information was uncovered by the *Milwaukee Journal Sentinel*, which reported that the Lynde and Harry Bradley Foundation paid Charles Murray almost $1 million over eight years to research and write the book (Kissinger, 1994). The significance of this information is that the Bradley Foundation is on the right of the political spectrum, and funds research with a politically conservative bent. This information is crucially important. When taken in relation to his affiliation with the American Enterprise Institute, the considerable level of support the Bradley Foundation provided to Charles Murray is highly suggestive that the research may not have been free of ideological predispositions and biases.

As we can see, newspapers and magazines can provide very useful information. Moreover, they are easy to access. Current issues can be purchased in print form or viewed on the web. Older issues are sometimes made available by the publications themselves on the web, but more often are accessible through web-based databases that are available through both university and many public libraries. In addition, it is often possible to purchase print copies of articles through vendors or the publications themselves.

Nevertheless, while newspapers and magazines can be very useful for identifying the newsworthy links between the ideology of research and its funding sources, they are less useful in revealing other values-related matters. Such issues as the kinds of articles traditional scholarly journals publish and the role of theoretical paradigms are simply not newsworthy. For these kinds of investigations, we need to look at other kinds of sources.

Web 2.0

The social networking functions of the web can be another useful source of information. It is widely acknowledged that the World Wide Web has radically altered the way we find information. A good deal of information that had previously been available only in the print media – and in some cases only at libraries – is now available to anyone with a computer and an internet connection. In addition, unlike printed material, when information needs updating it can be done instantaneously on the web by someone who is authorized to do so. In part for these reasons, the web has evolved into an accepted means of finding information. Indeed, we have in this chapter mentioned that it is a source of newspaper articles as well as an excellent way of verifying a journal's policy on peer review or an author's credentials. Additionally, as we saw in the last chapter, gray literature, which is a good source of alternative research, is often found on the web.

Still, despite the ease of locating and changing information found on the web, the standard webpage retains an essential characteristic of the traditional print media: it is a publication medium in which a reader reads what has been written by an author, and the contents can only be edited by the site's 'owner', who accesses it with a user name and password. However, the functionalities of the web have expanded in the last few years with the development of a new set of web technologies that gave birth to what is commonly called 'Web 2.0'.

What characterizes Web 2.0 is its interactivity, and this interactivity opens up new ways of disseminating information. When you look at a standard webpage, a newspaper article, the homepage of an organization or individual, or any other informational piece, the distinction between author and reader is clear. Web 2.0, however, blurs that distinction, in that the same individual may perform both roles on the same site. Included under this rubric are blogs, where people read what other people have written, ask questions or post their own materials on the topic of the blog, which may in turn be commented upon by others. Another example is wikis, the best-known instance of which is the encyclopedia Wikipedia (www.wikipedia.org). Wikis are webpages that are designed to be created and modified by multiple users. Sometimes the rights to modify a wiki are restricted to a particular group of people, but it is by definition collaborative: multiple users can contribute to a wiki as well as edit the work of other contributors. Some of this material may indeed be of a serious nature that does not get published in the standard venues.

What is of interest to us for the purposes of this book is not the technology, but the lack of external constraint on what is disseminated through mechanisms such as blogs and wikis. Suppose, for example, you are interested in the side-effects of SSRI (selective serotonin reuptake inhibitor) antidepressants such as Prozac. You have reviewed the literature, but wonder if the issue has been fully discussed in the material you have read. Under such circumstances, looking at blogs discussing antidepressants may prove useful.

One example of such a blog is 'Clinical psychology and psychiatry: a closer look' (http://clinpsyc.blogspot.com/), a site devoted to the role of psychiatry, psychiatric medications and marketing. You might note that in many postings people give personal accounts of prolonged sexual dysfunction they believe to be caused by SSRIs (http://clinpsyc.blogspot. com/2006/12/sexual-side-effects-of-ssris-even-more.html? showComment=1209897420000#c6813024032973232448). While these discussions do not constitute research, they can suggest that further investigation of the issue of SSRI side-effects may indeed be warranted – especially since data about negative sexual side-effects may be just the sort of thing a pharmaceutical company might not want to look at too closely.

On occasion, a blog can do more than simply raise red flags. It can sometimes point us to scholarly research that may prove invaluable in critical assessment. So, for example, one of the postings on the 'Clinical psychology and psychiatry' blog contains a reference to a scholarly article on the topic of the sexual side-effects of SSRI antidepressants (http://clinpsyc.blogspot.com/2008_05_01_archive.html). This well-documented article, by Audrey Bahrick (2008), points out that adverse persistent sexual side-effects of SSRI antidepressants occur at 'significantly higher' rates than those 'reported in pre-market trials and currently listed in the drug insert literature' (ibid.: 43). She further notes that the studies in question did not even specifically ask the patients about sexual side-effects, basing their conclusions instead solely on the spontaneous reports of patients. Reported rates of sexual dysfunction are much higher when patients are asked directly about these problems (ibid.). Bahrick's work suggests the underreporting of sexual side-effects in the research articles may be related to the financial interests of the pharmaceutical company research sponsors.

Scholarly sources

Articles

Scholarly publications are often the best way of finding information about other scholarly publications. The simplest way of looking for relevant journal articles is using the databases offered in all university and college libraries, and many public libraries as well. It is important to be aware that libraries pay substantial fees to subscribe to these databases. They are not freely available to the public in the way free websites are. They are, however, accessible at no charge to the library card-holders of public libraries and to the students, staff and faculty of an institution to which an academic library belongs. In some cases, unaffiliated users are welcome to come into the library and use the databases at no charge.

Still, it can sometimes appear to be far simpler to do a database search than it really is. How can you know which of the many databases available are relevant? Some databases offer a breakdown of the journals they contain by subject, and you can use these subject listings to see if the database you are considering actually has journals in the area in which you are interested. If you are looking for material on scientific aspects of pharmaceutical research, for example, looking at a database such as Project Muse is probably the wrong place to go since it focuses on humanities and social science research; ScienceDirect might be a better choice since it focuses on science.

Deciding on the best databases can be a time-consuming process and, in many cases, enlisting the help of a skilled librarian is a good idea. A knowledgeable librarian can help guide you through the vast and sometimes confusing array of database offerings and make your investigations much more effective.

Google Scholar (http://scholar.google.com), a free service which searches the scholarly literature, may be also be helpful. However, it is worth keeping in mind that although web searches using Google Scholar or any other search engine can identify scholarly articles, it is usually difficult to get the actual texts without paying for them. Once again, libraries can be very useful because they have the databases that can be used to access the texts of articles that are not otherwise available for free.

However, there is one source of scholarly literature which does not necessitate going to databases or paying money for copies of articles. Many people are not aware that some peer-reviewed research is published in open access journals that are available on the web free of charge. Many of these journals can be located through the *Directory of Open Access Journals* (www.doaj.org/), and the articles can be downloaded at no charge.

Before leaving the subject of scholarly articles, we should point out that sometimes, as we noted in Chapter 4, the core, standard academic publications are not always the best sources of information. At least at times, alternative scholarly publications may prove more useful in providing different perspectives. At the very least, we would strongly suggest not excluding journals simply because they are not the most established journals in a field. Sometimes straying from the well-worn paths can lead you to ideas, facts and perspectives you would not have encountered otherwise.

Books

In addition to scholarly articles, books can be an important source of information. To learn of works beyond your local library, it is often worth investigating larger catalogs such as WorldCat, the Library of Congress Catalog and the British Library Integrated Catalogue. All of these are available on the web free of charge. In fact, the catalogs of most libraries throughout the world are available now to the general public through the web. Even if your local library does not have the works you find this way, it might very well be able to get them through an interlibrary loan service.

Another way to find books is through Google Books (http://books.google.com/), which makes a substantial number of books available on the web to the general public without charge. When the entire book is not available, however, you can use Google Books in the same way as you would a library catalog and get access to the materials you want through a library.

Gray literature

To supplement scholarly books and articles, consider searching for relevant gray literature. We saw in the last chapter that significant data about the drug Celebrex, as compared with the older drugs that had been prescribed to treat arthritis, were disseminated as gray literature on the FDA website. The data on this site showed that the research findings published in *JAMA* did not include all the data from the study, a revelation that had major implications for conclusions about the safety of the drug. Indeed, Michael Wolfe, an editor of the highly prestigious medical journal *JAMA*, indicated that he would not have written a positive editorial about the published Celebrex study had he known of the existence of these data. That these data were omitted from a report on the findings of pharmaceutical-sponsored research suggests that financial interests may have been at least in part responsible for the omission.

The Celebrex case is by no means the only instance in which gray literature has proven an invaluable source for locating pure data that may reveal possible financial conflicts of interest. As far back as 1995, the 'smoking-gun' documents that exposed the tobacco industry's prior knowledge of the adverse health effects of tobacco were digitized and published on the internet at the library of the University of California at San Francisco (www.library.ucsf.edu/tobacco).

However, it is not only famous cases where gray literature becomes useful. As we noted in the last chapter, governments and foundations as well as individual scientists and scholars often post research on the web. This material can be found by doing a web search. Sometimes these materials can change our assessment of research dramatically.

How do you look for such material? Sometimes it is as simple as a web search in a standard search engine using keywords that describe the research topic. If one set of words does not yield relevant results, try another. If your search retrieves so much material that you cannot possibly review it all, try narrowing the search by restricting the search to domains that are likely to yield gray literature, more specifically to domains that are used by governments, non-profits and universities.

In the United States there are specific domain names that are used to denote different types of organization: .edu for educational sites, particularly higher education sites, .gov for government agencies and .org for non-profit organizations. In the United Kingdom, institutions of higher education are designated by .ac.uk, while government sites are identified by .gov.uk and non-profits by .org.uk. While there is some variation in these domains from country to country, it is often possible to use them to narrow the scope of your gray literature search to more manageable dimensions.

How do you narrow searches down to these areas? The easiest way is to go into the 'advanced search' facility in a standard search engine such as Google or Yahoo! In both of these search engines, and in many others as well, there is a box or slot that allows you to specify a particular domain.

Another trick to finding gray literature is to search for files intended for .pdf readers, since gray literature often appears in this format. Once again, advanced searches in standard search engines can be useful: they will often allow you to specify document type. However, even this is not always necessary, since in most cases adding '.pdf' as a search term even in a simple search will narrow the search sufficiently.

Beyond this point, identifying actual sources of data is often a matter of finding keywords that might be used on the relevant webpages. Terms describing the research topic and terms relating to research findings such as 'data', 'statistics' or 'tables' can all be useful search terms to tease out relevant gray literature. Still, it must be emphasized that serendipity can play an important role, and you should not be discouraged if searches at times come up with few or no useful results. Here, and in all other searches, willingness to approach the challenge playfully, trying different words and strategies, is essential.

Scholarly references

One important way of contextualizing research does not, in fact, involve searching at all. Rather, it exploits the fact that research does not take place in a vacuum. Researchers always refer back to previous work done on a topic and comment on the work of others focusing on the same issues. When assessing the strengths and weaknesses of research, keeping this in mind can provide an important advantage.

If you find a relevant article or book on a topic, you should always look at the works it mentions. For formal scholarly and scientific articles and books, this means looking at the footnotes, reference lists or bibliographies that scholarly works always include. They can provide a goldmine of information. In fact, although such documentation is often discussed as merely a way of giving credit and avoiding plagiarism, providing a research context for readers is one of its traditional major functions.

However, formal documentation is not the only way of identifying these contexts. Popular media accounts such as newspaper and magazine articles, as well as television and radio, often refer to other work when discussing a particular research finding. As we mentioned before, blogs and wikis sometimes do the same. If you are interested in assessing research, paying attention to these references can help you to identify issues and concerns that might otherwise escape your notice.

Striking the right balance

The importance of understanding that research operates within a context has been the central concern of this book. Although we have examined many cases in which research has failed to live up to the ideal of disinterested investigation, we do not intend to convey the message that research in general is either useless or hopelessly corrupted. To the contrary, we firmly believe that research is crucial to achieving an understanding of the issues and challenges that confront us in our daily lives. That said, we do not think it is wise to view research in a decontextualized way, as somehow divorced from the economic and belief systems of the real world. Researchers participate in these systems, as do the rest of us, and we have tried to show throughout this book that we can only understand the strengths and weaknesses of research by recognizing the role these systems play.

We would argue that it is wrong to assume that the context in which a work occurs has no influence on its conclusions. To the contrary, we have shown that in a variety of different kinds of research this context can play a crucial role. The political ideology of the sponsors of *The Bell Curve* research is quite relevant to contextualizing the conclusions of that work, especially when one considers, as we do in Chapter 4, that the hereditarian hypothesis on which it is based is only one possible theoretical paradigm for understanding the data. Similarly, although we often take the accounting reports on which so many financial decisions in modern life are made as research performed in a disinterested manner, the Enron scandal, and indeed the recent sub-prime mortgage debacle, may not have been possible if it were not for the fact that accounting research is performed by institutions and individuals that are to a great extent beholden to the very companies about which their reports are supposed to be providing disinterested information.

We could in a childlike way simply say that in such cases the research is bad. This, however, we must stress again, is missing the point. Since no research takes place in a vacuum and no research is immune to the influence of economic and belief systems, the real challenge is to understand the ways in which these systems may affect and limit the insights the research provides. It is this awareness we refer to when we speak of the contexualization of research. Research should not be simply – or simplistically – rejected just because the researchers, like the rest of us, exist in the real world and are affected by its concerns.

Those of us on the receiving end of research – and, once again, that includes all of us at different times – are continually bombarded with new research findings, findings that often contradict what we had previously accepted as proven fact. New research findings, for example, may point to environmental factors that contribute to the development of Alzheimer's disease, only to be 'disproven' by a later study that suggests a different regimen for warding off the disease. New research findings on how to educate children may suggest that older approaches are inadequate. Previously accepted dietary recommendations are replaced with substantially different ones that are based on the latest research. It is not unusual for people to express dismay, saying that every day they are confronted with different advice based on the latest research, and they no longer know what to think or how to respond.

How do we know when we should have confidence in research findings? Perhaps even more importantly, how do we know what we should be skeptical about?

What we are suggesting is really a philosophically conservative position. It suggests that we should not just rush to adopt the latest research findings and accept them uncritically as the newest truth, but rather consider them carefully, seeing how the conclusions have been influenced by their contexts and how that in turn may affect the ways in which the findings may be useful.

In a sense the gold standards that we have discussed serve to reinforce this conservative approach to evaluating research. The peer-review process and the emphasis placed on the expertise and credentials of the author – expertise that is recognized by the community of the author's peers – serve to uphold the standards to which research has traditionally been held. These standards serve as important quality control mechanisms. However, what the gold standards do not do is to consider fully the economic and belief systems that affect research. Indeed, one might argue that they are not set up to consider such factors at all, which is why we have seen in case after case that when one or another aspect of the economic or belief system affects research in untoward ways, the review process frequently does not prove to be an adequate corrective.

We are not suggesting systemic changes to the institutional ways in which research is vetted. Such proposals would be beyond the scope of this work. Our goal has been more modest. What we have attempted to do is to make readers more aware of some of the issues in the critical assessment of research that go beyond the gold standards, in the hope that this awareness will lead our readers to ask the probing questions that always need to be asked of research. While this awareness may not resolve in a systemic way any of the issues that have been noted in this study, without such awareness it is unlikely such systemic changes will ever be made.

References

Ahmed, N. (2005) '23 years of the discovery of *Helicobacter pylori*: is the debate over?', *Annals of Clinical Microbiology and Antimicrobials*, 4: 17–19; available at: *www.ann-clinmicrob.com/content/4/1/17* (accessed: 13 December 2008).

Alkalimat, A. (1986) *Introduction to Afro-American Studies: A Peoples College Primer*. Chicago, IL: Twenty-first Century Books and Publications.

American Enterprise Institute (2005) 'AEI's organization and purposes'; available at: *www.aei.org/about/filter.all/default.asp* (accessed: 9 November 2008).

American Enterprise Institute (2009a) 'History of AEI'; available at: *www.aei.org/history* (accessed: 11 May 2009).

American Enterprise Institute (2009b) 'Charles Murray'; available at: *www.aei.org/scholar/43* (accessed: 13 May 2009).

American Heart Association (2009) 'Publications and statistics'; available at: *www.americanheart.org/presenter.jhtml?identifier=3055922* (accessed: 28 May 2009).

American Institute of Certified Public Accountants (2009a) 'National Peer Review Committee (formerly known as the Center for Public Company Audit Firms) Peer Review Program'; available at: *www.aicpa.org/centerprp/index.htm* (accessed: 14 June 2009).

American Institute of Certified Public Accountants (2009b) *Professional Standards. U.S. Auditing Standards. Appendix A – Historical Background*. New York: AICPA; available at Accounting, Audit & Corporate Finance Library: *https://checkpoint.riag.com* (accessed: 16 April 2009).

American Institute of Certified Public Accountants (2009c) *Professional Standards. Applicability of AICPA Professional Standards and PCAOB Standards. Part I – Applicability of AICPA Professional*

Standards and Public Company Accounting Oversight Board Standards. New York: AICPA; available at Accounting, Audit & Corporate Finance Library: *https://checkpoint.riag.com* (accessed: 16 April 2009).

American Psychiatric Association (1973) 'Homosexuality and sexual orientation disturbance: proposed change in *DSM-II*', 6th printing, position statement (retired), APA Document Reference No. 730008; available at: *www.psychiatryonline.com/DSMPDF/DSM-II_ Homosexuality_Revision.pdf* (accessed: 9 June 2009).

Anderson, J.M. (2002) 'Enron: a select chronology of congressional, corporate, and government activities', Congressional Research Service Report for Congress. Received through the CRS Web.

Anheier, H.K. (2001) 'Foundations in Europe: a comparative perspective', Civil Society Working Paper 18; available at: *www.lse.ac.uk/collections/visionsAndRolesOfFoundationsInEurope/d ocuments.htm* (accessed: 18 February 2009).

Annals of Physics (2009) 'Peer review policy for *Annals of Physics*'; available at: *www.elsevier.com/wps/find/journaldescription.cws_ home/622784/preface1* (accessed: 11 January 2009).

Atwood, K.C. IV (2004) 'Bacteria, ulcers, and ostracism? *H. pylori* and the making of a myth', *Skeptical Inquirer*, November; available at: *www.csicop.org/si/200411/bacteria.html* (accessed: 3 December 2008).

Austin, A.E. (1916) 'Diagnosis of duodenal ulcer', *New York Medical Journal*, CIV: 984–8.

Bahrick, A.S. (2008) 'Persistence of sexual dysfunction side effects after discontinuation of antidepressant medications: emerging evidence', *Open Psychology Journal*, 1: 42–50.

Bailey, R. (2006) 'Science, normal science and science education – Thomas Kuhn and education', *Learning for Democracy*, 2(2): 7–20.

Baird, P. (2003) 'Getting it right: industry sponsorship and medical research', *Canadian Medical Association Journal*, 168(10): 1267–9.

Bakanic, V., McPhail, C. and Simon, R.J. (1987) 'The manuscript review and decision-making process', *American Sociological Review*, 52(5): 631–42.

Bantley, K.A. (2008) 'Judicial activism and progressive legislation: a step towards decreasing hate attacks', *Albany Law Review*, 71: 545–64.

Bazerman, M.H. and Watkins, M.D. (2004) *Predictable Surprises: The Disasters You Should Have Seen Coming, and How to Prevent Them*. Boston, MA: Harvard Business School Press.

Bearden, R. and Henderson, H. (1993) *A History of African American Artists: From 1792 to the Present*. New York: Pantheon Books.

Beckett, L.E. (2006) 'Greenblatt to be next "keeper of the canon"', *The Harvard Crimson*, 11 January; available at: *www.thecrimson.com/article.aspx?ref=510821* (accessed: 18 May 2009).

Binet, A. (1916) 'New methods for the diagnosis of the intellectual level of subnormals', translated by Elizabeth S. Kite, in *The Development of Intelligence in Children*. Baltimore, MD: Williams & Wilkins, pp. 37–90.

Block, N.J. (1995) 'How heritability misleads about race', *Cognition*, 56: 99–128.

Block, N.J. and Dworkin, G. (1974a) 'IQ: heritability and inequality, Part 1', *Philosophy and Public Affairs*, 3(4): 331–409.

Block, N.J. and Dworkin, G. (1974b) 'IQ: heritability and inequality, Part 2', *Philosophy and Public Affairs*, 4(1): 40–99.

Bloom, H. (1994) *The Western Canon: The Books and School of the Ages*. New York: Harcourt Brace.

Bombardier, C., Laine, L., Reicin, A., Shapiro, D. et al. (2000) 'Comparison of upper gastrointestinal toxicity of Rofecoxib and Naproxen in patients with rheumatoid arthritis', *New England Journal of Medicine*, 23 November, pp. 1520–8; available at *www.nejm.org* (accessed: 16 February 2009).

Bouchard, T.J. Jr (1995) 'Breaking the last taboo', *Contemporary Psychology*, 40(5); available at: *http://felix.unife.it/Root/dMensafiles/dIntelligence/tBellcurvereviews* (accessed: 3 November 2008).

Boxer, M.J. (2000) 'Unruly knowledge: women's studies and the problem of disciplinarity', *NWSA Journal*, 12(2): 119–29.

Boyd, C. (2004) 'The structural origins of conflicts of interest in the accounting profession', *Business Ethics Quarterly*, 14(3): 377–98.

Brawley, G.B. (1937) *Negro Genius: A New Appraisal of the Achievement of the American Negro in Literature and the Fine Arts*. New York: Biblo and Tannen.

Brimelow, P. (1994) 'For whom the bell tolls', *Forbes*, 154(10): 153–63.

Brody, H. (2007) *Hooked: Ethics, the Medical Profession, and the Pharmaceutical Industry*. Lanham, MD: Rowman & Littlefield.

Brookings Institution (undated) 'About Brookings'; available at: *www.brookings.edu/about.aspx* (accessed: 28 May 2009).

Bryan-Low, C. (2003) 'Accounting firms earn more from consulting – despite SEC crackdown, buying nonaudit services by companies stays high', *Wall Street Journal*, 16 April, p. C9.

Bryant, C.G.A. (1975) 'Kuhn, paradigms and sociology', *British Journal of Sociology*, 26(3): 354–9.

Cassel, C. (1952) 'The medical management of peptic ulcer', *American Journal of Nursing*, 52(7): 852–5.

Chan, S. and East, P. with Ali, S. and Neophytou, M, adapted and updated by Faulkner, K. (2004, 2008) *A Recent History of Primary and Secondary Education in England: Part 1: 1944 to 1985*. London: ITT.

Chandra, G. (2003) 'The Enron implosion and its lessons', *Journal of Management Research*, 3(2): 89–111.

Chang, K. (2004) 'Evidence on cold fusion remains inconclusive, new review finds', *New York Times*, 2 December, p. A31.

Chen, J.-Q. and Gardner, H. (1997) 'Alternative assessment from a multiple intelligences theoretical perspective', in D.P. Flanagan, J.L. Genshaft and P.L. Harrison (eds) *Contemporary Intellectual Assessment: Theories, Tests, and Issues*. New York: Guilford Press, pp. 105–21.

Christie, D.A. and Tansey, E.M. (eds) (2002) *Peptic Ulcer: Rise and Fall*. Transcript of Witness Seminar held at Wellcome Institute for the History of Medicine, London, 12 May 2000, *Wellcome Witnesses to Twentieth Century Medicine*, Vol. 14. London: Wellcome Trust Centre for the History of Medicine.

Çimen, F. (2008) 'Hittites' holy city Nerik to emerge', *Turkish Daily News*, 2 September.

City Journal (undated) 'About'; available at: *www.cityjournal.org/html/about_cj.html* (accessed: 10 November 2009).

Clark, J. (2003) 'A hot flush for Big Pharma: how HRT studies have got drug firms rallying the troops', *British Medical Journal*, 327: 400; available at: *www.bmj.com* (accessed: 3 November 2008).

Collier, J. and Iheanacho, I. (2002) 'The pharmaceutical industry as an informant', *The Lancet*, 360: 1405–9.

Colon, A. (2003) 'Black studies: historical background, modern origins, and development priorities for the early twenty first century', *Western Journal of Black Studies*, Fall; available at: *http://findarticles.com/p/articles/mi_go2877/is_3_27/ai_n7633058/?tag=content;col1* (accessed: 24 December 2008).

Connor, S. (2008) 'Drug giant Pfizer tries to force medical journal to reveal anonymous sources', *The Independent*, 10 March, p. 6.

Crowley, H. (1999) 'Women's studies: between a rock and a hard place or just another cell in the beehive?', *Feminist Review*, 61 (Spring),

Special Issue: Snakes and Ladders: Reviewing Feminisms at Century's End: 131–50.

De Cecco, J.P. (1987) 'Homosexuality's brief recovery: from sickness to health and back again', *Journal of Sex Research*, 23(1): 106–14.

de Groot, J. and Maynard, M. (eds) (1993) *Women's Studies in the 1990s: Doing Things Differently?* New York: St Martin's Press.

DeParle, J. (1990) 'Washington at work; an architect of the Reagan vision plunges into inquiry on race and I.Q.', *New York Times*, 30 November; available at: *www.nytimes.com* (accessed: 10 November 2008).

Dey, M. and Constantine, G.D. (2004) 'Wyeth: the leader in women's health – yesterday, today, and tomorrow', *Sexuality, Reproduction & Menopause*, 2(3): 181–4.

Dionne, E.J. Jr (1994) 'Race and IQ: stale notions…', *Washington Post*, 18 October, p. A17.

Dohrman, A.J. (2005) 'Rethinking and restructuring the FDA drug approval process in light of the Vioxx recall', *Journal of Corporation Law*, 31(1): 203–23.

Donadio, R. (2006) 'Keeper of the canon', *New York Times*, 8 January; available at: *www.nytimes.com* (accessed: 22 December 2008).

Dorfman, D.D. (1995) 'Soft science with a neoconservative agenda', *Contemporary Psychology*, 40(5); available at: *http://felix.unife. it/Root/dMensafiles/dIntelligence/tBellcurvereviews* (accessed: 3 November 2008).

Dow Jones News Service (2003) 'Pfizer, Pharmacia combine operations', Dow Jones News Service, 16 April.

Drazen, J.M. and Curfman, D.C. (2002) 'Financial associations of authors', *New England Journal of Medicine*, 346(24): 1901–2.

Drisceoil, D.Ó. (2005) '"The best banned in the land": censorship and Irish writing since 1950', *Yearbook of English Studies*, 35: 146–60.

Duff, O. (2006) 'David Irving: an anti-semitic racist who has suffered financial ruin', *The Independent*, 21 February; available at: *www.independent.co.uk/news/people/profiles* (accessed: 23 April 2009).

Eichenwald, K. (2005) *Conspiracy of Fools: A True Story*. New York: Broadway Books.

Elliott, K.C. (2008) 'Scientific judgment and the limits of conflict-of-interest policies', *Accountability in Research*, 15: 1–29.

Environmental News Network (2000) 'Science report: a third of U.S. schools don't teach evolution', CNN.com, 21 September; available at:

http://archives.cnn.com/2000/NATURE/09/21/evolution.enn/index.html (accessed: 22 September 2008).

Fancher, R.E. (1985) *The Intelligence Men, Makers of the I.Q. Controversy.* New York: W.W. Norton.

Fass, P.S. (1980) 'The IQ: a cultural and historical framework', *American Journal of Education*, 88(4): 431–58.

Fearnley, S., Beattie, V.A. and Brandt, R. (2005) 'Auditor independence and audit risk: a reconceptualization', *Journal of International Accounting Research*, 4(1): 39–71.

Felgran, H.M. and Hettinger, A. (2002) 'The wonder drug that wasn't', *Columbia Journalism Review*, September/October: 70–1.

Financial Reporting Council (2009a) 'Accounting Standards Board – welcome'; available at: *www.frc.org.uk/asb/* (accessed: 17 April 2009).

Financial Reporting Council (2009b) 'Professional Oversight Board. Audit Inspection Unit (AIU)'; available at: *www.frc.org.uk/pob/audit/* (accessed: 14 June 2009).

Finn, C. Jr (1995) 'For whom it tolls', *Commentary*, January: 76–80.

Flanagin, A., Fontanarosa, P.B. and DeAngelis, C.D. (2006) 'Update on *JAMA*'s conflict of interest policy', *Journal of the American Medical Association*, 296(2): 220–1.

Ford Foundation (2009) 'About us – our mission'; available at: *www.fordfound.org/about/mission* (accessed: 28 May 2009).

Galton, F. (1907) *Inquiries into Human Faculty and Its Development.* New York: E.P. Dutton.

Galton, F. (1962) *Hereditary Genius; An Inquiry into Its Laws and Consequences.* Cleveland, OH: Meridian Books.

Gardner, H. (1993) *Multiple Intelligences: The Theory in Practice.* New York: Basic Books.

Gelb, S.A. (1997) 'Heart of darkness: the discreet charm of the hereditarian psychologist', *Review of Education/Pedagogy/Cultural Studies*, 19(1): 129–39.

Gewertz, K. (2006) 'Greenblatt edits "Norton Anthology": eighth edition of collection of English lit published this month', *Harvard Gazette*; available at: *www.news.harvard.edu/gazette/2006/02.02/05-anth.html* (accessed: 9 June 2009).

Gibson, A. (1993) 'New approaches to art history', *American Art*, 7(2): 2–5.

Goldiner, D. (2008) 'Expert sees cancer tie to cell phones', *New York Daily News*, 31 March, p. 6.

Gouma-Peterson, T. and Mathews, P. (1987) 'The feminist critique of art history', *Art Bulletin*, 69(3): 326–57.

Govier, G. (2008) 'Finders of the lost ark, why some amateurs are stirring up dust and little else', *Christianity Today*, May: 62.

Gowers, A. (2006) *Gowers Review of Intellectual Property*. London: The Stationery Office; available at: *www.hm-treasury.gov.uk/d/pbr06_gowers_report_755.pdf* (accessed: 28 May 2009).

Greer, Germaine (1979) *The Obstacle Race: The Fortunes of Women Painters and Their Work*. New York: Farrar, Straus, Giroux.

GreyNet (2009) 'Grey Literature Network Service'; available at: *http://greynet.org/* (accessed: 25 May 2009).

Grob, G.N. (2003) 'The rise of peptic ulcer: 1900–1950', *Perspectives in Biology and Medicine*, 46(4): 550–66.

Gruber, H.E. (1974) *Darwin On Man: A Psychological Study of Scientific Creativity, Together With Darwin's Early and Unpublished Notebooks*, transcribed and annotated by Paul H. Barrett. New York: E.P. Dutton.

Hagaman, S. (1990) 'Feminist inquiry in art history, art criticism, and aesthetics: an overview for art education', *Studies in Art Education*, 32(1): 27–35.

Harper, R., Rodden, T., Rogers, Y. and Sellen, A. (2008) *Being Human: Human-Computer Interaction in the Year 2020*. Cambridge, MA: Microsoft Corporation; available at: *http://research.microsoft.com/en-us/um/cambridge/projects/hci2020/download.html* (accessed: 11 February 2009).

Hauser, R.M. (1995) '*The Bell Curve* by Richard J. Herrnstein [and] Charles Murray', *Contemporary Sociology*, 24(2): 149–53.

Healy, P.M. and Palepu, K.G. (2003) 'The fall of Enron', *Journal of Economic Perspectives*, 17(2): 3–26.

Herrington, D.M. (2003) 'Hormone replacement therapy and heart disease: replacing dogma with data', *Circulation*, 107: 2–4.

Herrnstein, R.J. and Murray, C. (1994) *The Bell Curve: Intelligence and Class Structure in American Life*. New York: Free Press.

Hibbard, H. (1980) *The Metropolitan Museum of Art*. New York: Harper & Row.

Hochman, M., Hochman, S., Bor, D. et al. (2008) 'News media coverage of medication research: reporting pharmaceutical company funding and use of generic medication names', *Journal of the American Medical Association*, 300(13): 1544–50.

Hogue, C.J. (2008) 'The triangular future of epidemiology', *Annals of Epidemiology*, 18(11): 862–4.

Holdcroft, A. (2007) 'Gender bias in research: how does it affect evidence based medicine?', *Journal of the Royal Society of Medicine*, 100: 2–3.

Hudson Institute (2009) 'About Hudson: William A. Schambra'; available at: *www.hudson.org/learn/index.cfm?fuseaction=staff_bio&eid=SchambraWill* (accessed: 13 May 2009).

Hulley, S., Grady, D., Bush, T. et al. (1998) 'Randomized trial of estrogen plus progestin for secondary prevention of coronary heart disease in postmenopausal women', *Journal of the American Medical Association*, 280(7): 605–13.

Hutcheon, P.D. (1996) 'Obscuring the message and killing the messenger: *The Bell Curve*', *Perspectives on Political Science*, 25(1): 15–18.

Ittenbach, R.F., Esters, I.G. and Wainer, H. (1997) 'The history of test development', in D.P. Flanagan, J.L. Genshaft and P.L. Harrison (eds) *Contemporary Intellectual Assessment: Theories, Tests, and Issues*. New York: Guilford Press, pp. 17–31.

Jackson, J.P. Jr (2006) '*Argumentum ad hominem* in the science of race', *Augmentation and Advocacy*, 43: 14–28.

Jacob, R. (1991) 'Can you trust that audit?', *Fortune*, 124(12): 191–4.

Jagose, A. (1996) *Queer Theory: An Introduction*. New York: New York University Press.

Jensen, A.R. (1969) 'How much can we boost IQ and scholastic achievement?', *Harvard Educational Review*, 39: 1–123.

Journal of English for Academic Purposes (2009) 'Peer review policy for the *Journal of English for Academic Purposes*'; available at: *www.elsevier.com/wps/find/journaldescription.cws_home/622440/preface1* (accessed: 11 January 2009).

Joyce, M. and Richardson, H. (1993) 'What is conservative philanthropy?', speech at Heritage Foundation, 11 March; available at: *www.policyarchive.org/bitstream/handle/10207/12659/92068_1.pdf?sequence=1* (accessed: 9 May 2009).

Kamin, L.J. (1974) *The Science and Politics of I.Q.* Potomac, MD: Lawrence Erlbaum Associates/Halsted Press.

Kaplan, R.L. (2004) 'The mother of all conflicts: auditors and their clients', *Journal of Corporation Law*, Winter: 363–83.

Katz, A. (2003) 'Observations and advertising: controversies in the prescribing of hormone replacement therapy', *Health Care for Women International*, 24: 927–39.

Kessler-Harris, A. (2007) 'Do we still need women's history?', *Chronicle of Higher Education*, 54(15): B6–B7.

King, R.T. Jr (1996) 'Bitter pill: how a drug firm paid for university study, then undermined it – research on thyroid tablets found cheap ones were just as good as sponsor's – article pulled at last minute', *Wall Street Journal*, 25 April, p. A1.

Kirkey, S. (2006) '"Cholesterol paradox" discovered: too low is also bad; heart failure study surprises researchers', *The Gazette (Montreal)*, 13 November, p. A11.

Kissinger, M. (1994) 'Explosive book on race has roots here. Bradley Foundation finances author whose theory on IQ has nation arguing', *Milwaukee Journal Sentinel*, 23 October.

Kolata, G. and Petersen, M. (2002) 'Hormone replacement study a shock to the medical system', *New York Times*, 10 July; available at: *www.nytimes.com* (accessed: 5 October 2008).

Koster, J. (2000) 'Variable-free grammar'; available at: *www.let.rug.nl/koster/papers/v-free.pdf* (accessed: 28 May 2009).

Koster, J. (2009) 'Some recent articles'; available at: *http://odur.let.rug.nl/~koster/1999.htm* (accessed: 28 May 2009).

Krafft-Ebing, R. von (1965) *Psychopathia Sexualis; A Medico-Forensic Study*, translated by Harry E. Wedeck. New York: Putnam.

Kramarae, C. and Spender, D. (eds) (1992) *The Knowledge Explosion: Generations of Feminist Scholarship*. New York: Teachers College Press.

Kranzler, J.H. (1995) 'Commentary on some of the empirical and theoretical support for *The Bell Curve*', *School Psychology Review*, 24(1): 36–41.

Krauthammer, C. (1994) 'IQ: what's the fuss?', *Washington Post*, 21 October, p. A25.

Kreisel, M. (1999) *American Women Photographers: A Selected and Annotated Bibliography*. Westport, CT: Greenwood Press.

Kuhn, T.S. (1962) *The Structure of Scientific Revolutions*. Chicago, IL: University of Chicago Press.

Lauter, P. (1991) *Canons and Contexts*. New York: Oxford University Press.

Lawry, S., Laurison, D. and VanAntwerpen, J. (2006) 'Liberal education and civic engagement: a project of the Ford Foundation's Knowledge, Creativity and Freedom Program'; available at: *www.fordfound.org/pdfs/impact/liberal_education_and_civic_engagement.pdf* (accessed: 21 February 2009).

Levine, L.W. (1996) *The Opening of the American Mind: Canons, Culture, and History*. Boston, MA: Beacon Press.

Levitt, A. (2002) 'Who audits the auditors?', *New York Times*, 17 January, Sec. A, p. 29.

Lichtenstein, D.R. and Wolfe, M.M. (2000) 'COX-2 – selective NSAIDs: new and improved?', *Journal of the American Medical Association*, 284(10): 1297–9.

Lilienfeld, S.O. (2002) 'When worlds collide: social science, politics, and the Rind et al. (1998) child sexual abuse meta-analysis', *American Psychologist*, 57(3): 176–88.

Lipstadt, D.E. (1993) *Denying the Holocaust: The Growing Assault on Truth and Memory*. New York: Free Press.

Lombardo, P.A. (2003) 'Pioneer's big lie', *Albany Law Review*, 66: 1125–44.

Machamer, P. (2009) 'Galileo Galilei', *Stanford Encyclopedia of Philosophy*; available at: *http://plato.stanford.edu/entries/galileo/* (accessed: 26 April 2009).

Magner, L.N. (1992) *A History of Medicine*. New York: M. Dekker.

Mailloux, S. (1978) 'Literary criticism and composition theory', *College Composition and Communication*, 29(3): 267–71.

Manhattan Institute for Policy Research (2009a) 'About'; available at: *www.manhattan-institute.org/html/about_mi_30.htm* (accessed: 7 June 2009).

Manhattan Institute for Policy Research (2009b) 'Announcing new book'; available at: *www.manhattan-institute.org/onenation_onestandard/* (accessed: 7 June 2009).

Manhattan Institute for Policy Research (2009c) 'Richard A. Epstein'; available at: *www.manhattaninstitute.org/html/epstein.htm* (accessed: 7 June 2009).

Mark Ware Consulting (2008) 'Peer review in scholarly journals: perspective of the scholarly community – an international study', Publishing Research Consortium; available at: *www.publishingresearch.net/documents/PeerReviewFullPRCReport-final.pdf* (accessed: 12 January 2009).

Marquis Who's Who on the Web (2009) New Providence, NJ: Marquis; available at: *www.marquiswhoswho.com/index.asp* (accessed: 7 June 2009).

Martin, J.L.R., Pérez, V., Sacristán, M. and Álvarez, E. (2005) 'Is grey literature essential for a better control of publication bias in psychiatry? An example from three meta-analyses of schizophrenia', *European Psychiatry*, 20: 550–3.

Marx, K. (1990) *Capital: A Critique of Political Economy*, 3 vols, translated by Ben Fowkes (vol. 1) and David Fernbach (vols 2 and 3). New York: Penguin Books in association with New Left Review.

McAuley, L., Pham, B., Tugwell, P. and Moher, D. (2000) 'Does the inclusion of grey literature influence estimates of intervention effectiveness reported in meta-analyses?', *The Lancet*, 356: 1228–31.

McCarthy, M. (1997) 'Sponsors lose fight to stop thyroxine study publication', *The Lancet*, 349(9059): 1149.

McKee, L. (2008) 'Plankton offer rare good news in global warming', *Belfast Telegraph*, 24 September, p. 42.

McLean, B. (2001) 'Is Enron overpriced?', *Fortune*, 5 March; available at: *http://money.cnn.com/2006/01/13/news/companies/enronoriginal_fortune/* (accessed: 17 March 2009).

Meyerowitz, L. (1997) 'The Negro in Art Week: defining the "new negro" through art exhibition', *African American Review*, 31(1): 75–89.

Montague, J.B. Jr (1959) 'Some problems of selection for secondary schools in England – implications for the U.S.', *Journal of Educational Sociology*, 32(8): 374–8.

Moynihan, R. (2003) 'Drug company secretly briefed medical societies on HRT', *British Medical Journal*, 326: 1161; available at: *www.bmj.com* (accessed: 8 October 2008).

New York Times (1994) 'The "Bell Curve" agenda', *New York Times*, 24 October, p. A16.

Newmeyer, F.J. (1986) 'Has there been a "Chomskyan Revolution" in linguistics?', *Language*, 62(1): 1–18.

Nochlin, L. (1988) *Women, Art, and Power: And Other Essays*. New York: Harper & Row.

Oaks, R.F. (1978) '"Things fearful to name": sodomy and buggery in seventeenth-century New England', *Journal of Social History*, 12(2): 268–81.

Okie, S. (2001) 'Missing data on Celebrex; full study altered picture of drug', *Washington Post*, 5 August, p. A11.

Oliver, D.T. (1998) 'The most generous big foundations: who are they?', *Alternatives in Philanthropy*, June: 1–10.

Palmlund, I. (2006) 'Loyalties in clinical research on drugs: the case of hormone replacement therapy', *Social Science & Medicine*, 63: 540–51.

Pattullo, E.L. (1996) '*The Bell Curve: Intelligence and Class Structure in American Life*: books in review', *Society*, 33(3): 86–8.

Pioneer Fund (undated.a) 'About us'; available at: *www.pioneerfund. org/* (accessed: 12 November 2008).

Pioneer Fund (undated.b) 'Grantees'; available at: *www. pioneerfund.org/Grantees.html* (accessed: 12 November 2008).

Prince, J. (2004) 'Queer history, this: an American synthesis', *Culture, Society & Praxis*, 3(1): 60–3.

Public Oversight Board (2001) 'Charter'; available at: *www.publicoversightboard.org/charter.htm* (accessed: 14 June 2009).

Rabin, S. (2005) 'Nicolaus Copernicus', *Stanford Encyclopedia of Philosophy*; available at: *http://plato.stanford.edu/entries/copernicus/* (accessed: 5 June 2009).

Rashid, R. (2009) 'Letter from Rick Rashid', Microsoft Research – Advancing the Frontiers of Computing; available at: *http://research.microsoft.com/en-us/about/brochure-1.aspx* (accessed: 28 May 2009).

Richardson, K. and Bynner, J.M. (1984) 'Intelligence: past and future', *International Journal of Psychology*, 19: 499–526.

Rick, J., O'Regan, S. and Kinder, A. (2006) *Early Intervention Following Trauma: A Controlled Longitudinal Study at Royal Mail Group*. Brighton: Institute for Employment Studies; available at: *www.bohrf.org.uk/downloads/traumrpt.pdf* (accessed: 28 May 2009).

Robert Bosch Stiftung (undated.a) 'Mission and establishment'; available at: *www.bosch-stiftung.de/content/language2/html/3290.asp* (accessed: 28 May 2009).

Robert Bosch Stiftung (undated.b) 'Start page'; available at: *www.bosch-stiftung.de/content/language2/html/index.asp* (accessed: 28 May 2009).

Rogers, A.I. (1997) 'Celebrating 50 years of *Postgraduate Medicine*; peptic ulcer disease', *Postgraduate Medicine*, 102(5): 158.

Roscoe, W. (1995) 'Strange craft, strange history, strange folks: cultural amnesia and the case for lesbian and gay studies', *American Anthropologist* New Series, 97(3): 448–53.

Rothman, S.M. and Rothman, D.J. (2003) *The Pursuit of Perfection: The Promise and Perils of Medical Enhancement*. New York: Pantheon Books.

Routledge, Taylor & Francis Group (2007) 'Information for authors'; available at: *www.routledge.com/info/authors* (accessed: 21 April 2009).

Rove, K. (2006) 'Karl Rove at American Enterprise Institute', 15 May; available at: *www.washingtonpost.com/wp-dyn/content/article/2006/05/15/AR2006051500635.html* (accessed: 7 June 2009).

Rushton, J.P. (2002) 'The Pioneer Fund and the scientific study of human differences', *Albany Law Review*, 66: 207–62.

San Diego State University (2006) 'Women's studies timeline'; available at: *www.rohan.sdsu.edu/dept/wsweb/timeline.htm* (accessed: 18 May 2009).

Saul, S. (2008) 'Setback for effort to ease rules on promoting drugs', *New York Times*, 19 April, p. C3.

Schambra, W. (2008) 'Conservative philanthropy: tactics and vision', prepared remarks given at the Colorado Association of Foundations Workshop on Advocacy, 12 September; available at: *www.hudson.org/files/publications/2008_09_12_Schambra_on_Fundi ng_Advocacy.pdf* (accessed: 9 May 2009).

Schwartz, P. (2002) '"Women's studies, gender studies": le contexte américain', *Vingtième Siècle. Revue d'histoire*, 75: 15–20.

Selye, H. (1976) *The Stress of Life*. New York: McGraw-Hill.

Silverstein, F.E., Faich, G., Goldstein, J.L. et al. (2000) 'Gastrointestinal toxicity with celecoxib vs nonsteroidal anti-inflammatory drugs for osteoarthritis and rheumatoid arthritis: the CLASS study: a randomized controlled trial. Celecoxib Long-term Arthritis Safety Study', *Journal of the American Medical Association*, 284(10): 1247–55.

Smith, S. (2003) 'Hormone therapy's rise and fall, science lost its way, and women lost out', *Boston Globe*, 20 July, p. A1.

Sowell, T. (1995) 'Ethnicity and IQ', *American Spectator*, 28(2): 32–7.

Spearman, C. (1904) 'Objectively determined and measured', *American Journal of Psychology*, 15(2): 201–92.

Spiro, H.M. (1998) 'Peptic ulcer: Moynihan's or Marshall's disease?', *The Lancet*, 352(9128): 645.

Stein, E. (1999) *The Mismeasure of Desire: The Science, Theory, and Ethics of Sexual Orientation*. New York: Oxford University Press.

Stern, N. (2007) *The Economics of Climate Change: The Stern Review*. Cambridge: Cambridge University Press.

Sternberg, R.J. (1995) 'For whom the bell curve tolls: a review of *The Bell Curve*', *Psychological Science*, 6(5): 257–61.

Sternberg, R.J., Grigorenko, E.L. and Kidd, K.K. (2005) 'Intelligence, race, and genetics', *American Psychologist*, 60(1): 46–59.

Tetreault, M.K.T. (1985) 'Feminist phase theory: an experience-derived evaluation model', *Journal of Higher Education*, 56(4): 363–84.

Thomas, C.W. (2002) 'Rise and fall of Enron', *Journal of Accountancy*, January; available at: *www.journalofaccountancy.com* (accessed: 14 October 2008).

Thompson, J.B. (2005) *Books in the Digital Age: The Transformation of Academic and Higher Education Publishing in Britain and the United States.* Cambridge: Polity Press.

Thorndike, E.L. (1920) 'The reliability and significance of tests of intelligence', *Journal of Educational Psychology*, 11(5): 284–7.

Thorndike, E.L. (1921) 'On the organization of intellect', *Psychological Review*, 28(2): 141–51.

Thorndike, R.M. (1997) 'Early history of intelligence testing', in D.P. Flanagan, J.L. Genshaft and P.L. Harrison (eds) *Contemporary Intellectual Assessment: Theories, Tests, and Issues.* New York: Guilford Press, pp. 3–16.

Time (1970) 'Black studies: a painful birth', *Time*, 26 January; available at: *www.time.com* (accessed: 24 December 2008).

Toffler, B.L. (2003) *Final Accounting: Ambition, Greed, and the Fall of Arthur Andersen.* New York: Broadway Books.

Tucker, W.H. (1994) 'Fact and fiction in the discovery of Sir Cyril Burt's flaws', *Journal of the History of the Behavioral Sciences*, 30: 335–47.

Turner, E.H., Matthew, A.M., Linardatos, E. et al. (2008) 'Selective publication of antidepressant trials and its influence on apparent efficacy', *New England Journal of Medicine*, 358: 252–60.

University at Buffalo Libraries (undated) 'Evaluating resources: periodicals'; available at: *http://library.buffalo.edu/asl/tutorials/evaluating_periodicals.html* (accessed: 11 January 2009).

US Centers for Disease Control and Prevention (1997) 'Knowledge about causes of peptic ulcer disease', *MMWR Weekly*, 46(42): 985–7; available at: *www.cdc.gov/mmwr/preview/mmwrhtml/00049679.htm* (accessed: 2 December 2008).

US Centers for Disease Control and Prevention (2006) 'History of ulcer diagnosis and treatment: *Helicobacter pylori* and peptic ulcer disease'; available at: *www.cdc.gov/ulcer/history.htm* (accessed: 2 December 2008).

US Congress Office of Technology Assessment (1988) *New Developments in Biotechnology: U.S. Investment in Biotechnology – Special Report, OTA-BA-360.* Washington, DC: US Government Printing Office.

US General Accounting Office (2002) *Financial Statement Restatements: Trends, Market Impacts, Regulatory Responses, and Remaining Challenges*, report to the Chairman, Committee on Banking, Housing, and Urban Affairs, US Senate. Washington, DC: US Government Printing Office.

US Senate Committee on Governmental Affairs (2002) 'Financial oversight of Enron: the SEC and private-sector watchdogs: report of the staff to the Senate Committee on Governmental Affairs'; available at: *http://hsgac.senate.gov/100702watchdogsreport.pdf* (accessed: 16 October 2008).

Vogel, G. (1997) 'Long-suppressed study finally sees light of day', *Science*, 276(5312): 523–5.

Warner, T.D. and Gluck, J.P. (2003) 'What do we really know about conflicts of interest in biomedical research?', *Psychopharmacology*, 171: 36–46.

Wilson, P. (1983) *Second-hand Knowledge: An Inquiry into Cognitive Authority*. Westport, CT: Greenwood Press.

Wilson, P.W., Garrison, R.J. and Castelli, W.P. (1985) 'Postmenopausal estrogen use, cigarette smoking, and cardiovascular morbidity in women over 50. The Framingham Study', *New England Journal of Medicine*, 313(17): 1038–43.

Wilson, R.A. (1962) 'The roles of estrogen and progesterone in breast and genital cancer', *Journal of the American Medical Association*, 182(4): 327–31.

Wilson, R.A. (1966) *Feminine Forever*. New York: Evans.

Wright, J.M. (2002) 'The double-edged sword of COX-2 selective NSAIDs', *Canadian Medical Association Journal*, 167(10): 1131–7.

Writing Group for the Women's Health Initiative Investigators (2002) 'Risks and benefits of estrogen plus progestin in healthy postmenopausal women: principal results from the Women's Health Initiative randomized controlled trial', *Journal of the American Medical Association*, 288(3): 321–33; available at: *http://jama.ama-assn.org/cgi/content/full/288/3/321* (accessed: 4 May 2009).

Index